Emerson: Prophecy, Metamorphosis, and Influence

Selected Papers from the English Institute

EMERSON: PROPHECY,

METAMORPHOSIS, AND

INFLUENCE

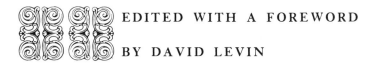 EDITED WITH A FOREWORD

BY DAVID LEVIN

Columbia University Press · New York and London · 1975

Library of Congress Cataloging in Publication Data
English Institute.
  Emerson—prophecy, metamorphosis, and influence.
  Papers from two sessions of the English Insti-
tute, held in 1973 and 1974.
  Includes bibliographical references.
  1. Emerson, Ralph Waldo, 1803–1882—Addresses,
essays, lectures. I. Levin, David, 1924– II. Title.
PS1631.E55   1975   814'.3   75-17704
ISBN 0-231-04000-8

Acknowledgment is made to Oxford University Press for permission
to print Harold Bloom's essay "The Freshness of Transformation:
Emerson's Dialectics of Influence," from *A Map of Misreading* by
Harold Bloom. Copyright © 1975 by Oxford University Press, Inc.
Reprinted by permission.
Acknowledgment is made to Harvard University Press for permission to print Albert Gelpi's essay "Emerson: The Paradox of
Organic Form," from *The Tenth Muse: The Psyche of the American Poet*
by Albert Gelpi. © 1975 by the President and Fellows of Harvard
College.
Acknowledgment is made to Yale University Press for permission to
print Sacvan Bercovitch's essay "Emerson the Prophet: Romanticism, Puritanism, and Auto-American-Biography," from *The Puritan Origins of the American Self* by Sacvan Bercovitch. Copyright ©
1975 by Yale University.

Foreword

RALPH WALDO EMERSON claimed the right to emulate his Puritan ancestors in at least one way, even as he repudiated their authority. By seeing God and nature "face to face" rather than through his ancestors' eyes, he wanted to "enjoy an original relation to the universe." That famous line stands as a warning to all American scholars, especially to those inclined to study Emerson himself. All the contributors to this volume recognize in one way or another the comical implications of extensively studying such a mind as Emerson's, whose most memorable utterances declare the independence of the living from the dead. Why, Emerson asks, "should we grope among the dry bones of the past, or put the living generation into masquerade out of its faded wardrobe? The sun shines today also. There is more wool and flax in the fields. There are new lands, new men, new thoughts. Let us demand our own works and laws and worship."

Perhaps more than any other major American writer, Emerson has steadily drawn as much attention to his effect on others as to his own quality and practice. Ever since Andrews Norton wrote *A Discourse on the Latest Form of Infidelity* and Nathaniel Hawthorne deplored the most peculiar of the imitators who flocked to Concord in the 1840's, one major theme of commentary on Emerson has expressed concern for his influence, whether he has been praised as a liberator or denounced as a seducer. To those who lament his influence as a compounding of Maule's Curse or as an establishment of the Imperial Self, the question of their own completeness in describing Emerson's ideas has not seemed very important. He could be quoted against himself on many issues, but the question remains: What pernicious effect did his most seductive ideas and attitudes have on the lives and work of successors?

In a sense, then, the concern of the following essays with Emerson's influence and development does not violate the spirit of his demand for originality. The implicit questions become: What does he mean to us? What can we make of him now? How does he help us to understand our own time? These questions are prominent not only in Harold Bloom's discussion of the anxiety of influence and in Albert Gelpi's delineation of an Emersonian tradition, but also in the essays by Sacvan Bercovitch, James M. Cox, Phyllis Cole, and Daniel B. Shea. The papers by Professors Bloom, Cox, and Gonnaud were read at the 1973 session of the English Institute, directed by Sacvan Bercovitch, and the one problem on which they had all been asked to touch was that of the imperial self. (Quentin Anderson, author of *The Imperial Self*, was present at the 1973 session.) For the 1974 session, which I directed, Professors Gelpi, Cole, and Shea had copies of the 1973 papers; although they were not obliged to address themselves to controversy, several remarkable affinities among the seven essays justify their inclusion in a single volume, both for what they say about Emerson and for their revelation of critical preferences in our own time.

All these scholars address questions of origin, development, influence. All pay some attention to the quality of "doubleness" in Emerson, to the fullness or complexity, the compensations (if not the contradictions) in his thought. In two very important essays Bercovitch and Shea deepen our knowledge of Emerson's relation to Puritan tradition in both literature and theology, and their mutual interest in spiritual autobiography and the American mission relates their essays to those of Gelpi, Bloom, and Cox. Phyllis Cole, Shea, and Cox all focus intently on the issue of changes in Emerson himself, and from a European perspective Maurice Gonnaud shades in darker lines of awareness than he finds in Anderson's portrayal of the imperial self. At the center of the volume I have placed Shea, Cox, and Cole, all of whom concentrate on Emerson the writer, the significance and texture of his metaphors, and their changing form. At the end I have placed Bloom and Gelpi, who concentrate most emphatically upon Emerson's influence. Shea, Cox, and Bloom recognize Emerson's powerful ambition, and almost all these essays call our attention to the Emerson of "Experience" and "Fate," who knew something of alienation and mortality. One of Cox's chief contentions is that Emerson knew those grim qualities, and the power of illusion, early as well as late.

These are scholarly, critical essays, but several of them are also decidedly personal statements, faithful in their various ways to the example of Emerson. In the witty metaphors of Shea, the historical range of Shea and Bercovitch, the impassioned voice of Cox's later pages, the prophetic language of Bloom, we find evidence that our scholars have not only analyzed but heard the man who praised Montaigne's language for being "vascular and alive."

DAVID LEVIN

Charlottesville, Va.
February 10, 1975

Contents

Sacvan Bercovitch

EMERSON THE PROPHET: ROMANTICISM,

PURITANISM, AND AUTO-AMERICAN-BIOGRAPHY

AMERICA, . . . A VAST UNREAL, INTERMEDIARY THING. . . .
                            D. H. LAWRENCE, *Letters*

BEING AN AMERICAN IS NOT SOMETHING TO BE INHERITED SO MUCH
AS SOMETHING TO BE ACHIEVED. . . . THEN, WHY ARE WE SO
NERVOUS? WHY DO WE SO WORRY ABOUT OUR IDENTITY?
                            PERRY MILLER, *Nature's Nation*

IN *The Anxiety of Influence*, Harold Bloom describes the British and American Romantics as the common heirs to "a severely displaced Protestantism"; but "British poets swerve from their precursors," he observes, "while American poets labor to 'complete' their fathers." [1] The contrast seems to me a compelling cultural as well as literary insight. It directs us to Emerson as the central figure of the American Renaissance; it recalls the strong prophetic strain in Emerson's thought; and for my present purpose most importantly, it suggests that the long foreground to Emerson the prophet is the legacy of the colonial Puritan fathers.

[1] Bloom, *The Anxiety of Influence* (New York, 1973), pp. 152, 68. I would like to thank Myra Jehlin for her extremely perceptive and helpful reading of this essay.

The Puritan emphasis on prophecy is well known. From the start, the emigrants made the Book of Revelation a proof-text of the New England Way. Their outlook followed the premises of Reformed millennialism, but they went one step further. As visible saints on a social mission, they identified their progress with the progress of the church. European Protestants, from Luther through Foxe, were careful to distinguish between social and sacred identity. When they boasted of "national election" they used the concept metaphorically, to denote the provisional, latter-day conjunction of secular and redemptive history. The American Puritans changed metaphor to fact. They regarded their commonwealth, their locale, and their national covenant as being literally part of God's grand design. The New World and the remnant now arrived to redeem it were sacred as well as worldly facts. They represented the fulfillment of scriptural promises. In the settlers' formulaic phrase, they were types embossed upon the spiral of salvational time. History for them was prophecy postdated, and prophecy, history antedated. On these grounds, during the first decades, they fused personal and federal eschatology, the saint's preparation for heaven and the theocracy's march toward New Jerusalem. On these grounds, in defiance of exegetical convention, they recast the modern world as a setting for Armageddon: England as a second Babylon, ripe for the slaughter; America as the wilderness that was to blossom as the rose; all other peoples—in Asia, Africa, Europe, places still unknown or undiscovered—as spiritual dependencies, awaiting the completion of their errand. And on these grounds, toward the end of the century, the dwindling orthodoxy refused to abandon the fathers' ideal. In the face of an untoward present, they guaranteed the future by sustaining the rhetoric of the past. In effect, they rescued the venture by appropriating it to themselves. Interweaving autobiography and sacred history, they confirmed their role as prophets by asserting the communal purpose, and proved the continuity of purpose by the presence of their vision.

They compared themselves in this respect with the Old Testament seers; but again, their concept of an *American* mission impelled them toward a distinctive prophetic mode. Jeremiah derives his authority from tradition. The myth he represents is the commemorative expression of his race. His function as communal spokesman builds on the conflict between vision and fact; and accordingly, his outlook is dialectical, insistent on the irreconcilable dualism of what his people are and what they ought to be. The very need for prophecy, that is, arises out of an engagement with history and community; the very concept of fulfillment centers on the *problem* of the present. Even as he outlines the paradise to come, Jeremiah invokes the myth in terms of contradiction. He appeals to the past in order to call attention to the hiatus between fathers and sons. His representative stature, the authority both of his denunciations and of his predictions, is that of a tradition at odds with the course of history.

The prophetic outlook of the latter-day Puritan theocrats serves to obviate the contradiction. Cotton Mather earns his authority as communal spokesman not by his connection with any existent community, but by personal assertion. His myth is essentially projective and elite, the invention of expatriate idealists who declared themselves the party of the future, and then proceeded, in an astonishing act of will and imagination, to impose prophecy upon history. The first generations did not fully realize the potential of their rhetoric. Concerned as they were with building their city on a hill, they could not afford to disregard realities altogether. To some extent at least they had to confront the conflicts inherent in their venture. Mather's works show no such tension. His *Magnalia Christi Americana* seeks above all to

confirm its author's representative stature. Mather intended it to
be an epic history, and he referred constantly to earlier epics,
especially those of Virgil and Milton. But Latium and Eden
come to us from an irrevocable past. Like Jeremiah, Milton and
Virgil use prophecy to suggest the inadequacies of the present.
Mather locates his golden age in the future, and so conceives of
America heuristically, as microcosm of the world-wide work of
redemption and macrocosm of the redemptive work underway
in its representative consciousness. Insofar as he berates his contemporaries for backsliding, he dissociates them from the country's "true history." Raising the process of fulfillment entirely
into the realm of the imagination, he offers *himself*, the coherence
of *his* vision, as the link between the promise and its realization.

Mather's method issues in a peculiarly self-contained concept of heroism. Traditionally, the epic hero culminates the
myth-making process. Thus he serves to remind his imitators of
their *in*completeness; the transcendent model toward which they
aspire accentuates their own limiting historical conditions. The
Magnalia's heroes, on the contrary, delineate the myth in process. Considered in context, they are successive harbingers of
the Theopolis Americana at hand; each of them, in his distinctive historical situation, emerges as an emblem of destiny manifest. The retrospective *imitatio Christi* therefore opens into a de-
velopmental scheme, a sort of relay race toward eternity, where
the participants are essentially the same (all one in Christ), while
temporally they represent ascending stages of perfection. The
sons, Mather tells us, improve upon the fathers, as the New
Israel improves upon the Old, or "as a snowball, the *further* it
rolls, the *bigger* it grows." To identify with (say) John Winthrop,
"the American Nehemiah," is not merely to assume the charac-
teristics of a life finished and justified. It is this too, but more
largely it is to become part of a teleology. For Mather, the fa-

thers are prophetic exemplars, and he a greater Nehemiah, who would define us, as Americans, in relation to the still-unfolding New World *magnalia*, somewhere midway between the theocratic garden of God and its consummation in the paradise to be regained. And wherever the midway point falls in that visionary "inter-Sabbatical line," the status of representative American designates a comprehensive social-divine selfhood that by definition surmounts the contradictions of secular time.[2]

This concept of intermediate identity, in which self-perfection becomes synonymous with corporate progress, may be traced throughout the eighteenth and nineteenth centuries. In one form or another, it recurs in every form of national self-definition (the dream, the American mission, the redemptive West). It underlies the ambivalence toward the Puritans, as founding fathers *against* whom the sons measure their moral and political advance. It lends a special cast to American views of the "course of empire," of reform, technology, utopia, and the self-made man. It links Puritan chiliasm with Revivalist and Revolutionary post-millennialism. And (to return to my subject) it provides a clue to the character of Emerson's "severely displaced Protestantism." In a famous passage, Augustine describes theological displacement as the *"experimentum medietatis,"* [3] a "trial of the center," when the natural will overcomes the divine. The Puritans applied this concept to the false pilgrim's regress from Christ to the self; following Augustine, they found their main

[2] See my "Horologicals to Chronometricals," *Literary Monographs*, ed. E. Rothstein, no. 3 (Madison, 1970), pp. 41 ff.; "Cotton Mather," in *Major Writers of Early American Literature*, ed. E. Emerson (Madison, 1972), pp. 140–44; and "Nehemias Americanus," *Early American Literature*, VIII (1974), 220–38.

[3] Augustine, *De Trinitate*, in *Patrologia . . . Series Latinae*, ed. J. P. Migne, 221 vols. (Paris, 1844–80), XLII, 1006.

examples in Lucifer and Prometheus. The Romantics, we might say, redefined the *experimentum medietatis* as a victory of the soul. They undertook a Promethean journey that ascended *through* the Center of Indifference to an affirmation of the self as divinity incarnate. The development begins in England as early as the seventeenth century: with the Puritan "vulgar prophets" who arrogated the Godhead to themselves, with the Quaker notion of the inner light, with Milton's *De Doctrina Christiana* which announces that all believers are no less than Jesus sons of God. The line leads forward to the Romantics of our own time—to Carl Jung, for example, who warns us not to imitate Christ, since, properly seen, the self is God; or earlier, to Nietzsche, who advised man simply to forget God, love himself through self-generated grace, and thereby enact in himself the entire work of redemption.

So considered, the connection between Puritan and Romantic may be briefly stated. The Reformers, having unleashed the individual, doctrinally, through the principle of *sola fides*, the primacy of personal faith, found their defence against subjectivism in the principle of *sola scriptura*, the absolute authority of scripture. By that authority, they legislated the spiritual meaning of all facts—historical, experiential, natural, and above all the fact of the self. Every believer had to find his own way to God, but his success depended upon his capacity, by grace, to purge his inherent discrete identity and transform himself into an *exemplum fidei*, a christic emblem of the faith. He received the right to interpret, that is, by first interpreting himself in accordance with a shared biblical absolute. The Romantics displaced the entire structure simply by reversing the equation. They subsumed the concept of *exemplum fidei* under the principle of *sola fides*. Rendering subjectivism the touchstone of faith, they freed the individual to choose (or invent) his identity, and then to impose his own patterns upon experience, history, nature, Christ Himself.

In this context, it seems all but inevitable that the Romantic should be overwhelmed by the anxiety of influence. His imitation of Christ was a process of duplicating himself, fashioning emblems of faith in his own image—a deific creation *ex imaginatione* in which *caritas* depended on autonomy, and plenitude was narcissism extended to infinity. Accordingly, the precursor poet assumed the role formerly held by the tenacious natural self. The Puritan's dilemma was that the way from the self necessarily led through the self; history was part of the dialectic through which he had to overcome history. Sometimes the struggle became so severe that he could resolve it only by abandoning hope, or else (like the proto-Romantics just mentioned) by leaping, self and all, directly to Christ. For the Romantic, the way to the self led through the precursor poet. Only the strongest did not abandon either poetry or the self.

No Romantic voiced the need to persist more eloquently than Emerson did; and yet in public at least he subsumed anxiety in an assured external design. The influence he felt came, buoyantly, from national prospects. When he considered the advantages of experience, he spoke not only of the apocalypse of the mind, but, more largely, of national destiny. With all Romantics, he shifted the center of inspiration from the Bible to nature. But like his forebears he conflated secular and sacred identity, rendering eschatology a function of teleology. The grand sentiment, he wrote, "which the geography of America inevitably inspires," proves that "the truly Human . . . exists for us, shines in on us unawares. . . . One thing is plain for all men of common sense and common conscience, that here, here in America, is the home of man." What makes this plain is not the men *in* America, but man *as* America, and America not as a state of mind but, specifically and uniquely, as the New World landscape, the Bible's *littera-allegoria* become American *natura-prophetica*. It is crucial to Emerson's great essay on nature that "Prospects," its final section, speaks directly to "the American . . . in his own country," that it presents its Orphic "prophecy" through the medium of a New England bard, and that its famous closing appeal, "Build therefore your own world," returns us to the essay's opening invocation to "new lands, new men, new thoughts." The European symbolist interpreted creation as part of his *Bildungsbiographie*, since he himself, in Carlyle's words, was the "Messias of Nature." [4] Emerson's model of spiritual growth gathered meaning by its proleptic identification with the New World *telos*, of which the land itself was the prophecy—fact and promise entwined.

In short, the self Emerson sought was not only his but America's, or rather, in a unique blend of hermeneutics and symbolism, his as America's, and therefore America's as his. Erich Auerbach has noted that the *figura* differs from the symbol in that it refers us to an a priori historical design. "As we proceed from the thing to the thing signified," warns William Whitaker, the great Reformed exegete, "*we* bring no new sense, but only bring to light what was before concealed [by God] in the sign." The symbol, on the other hand, emerges through the direct interaction between perceiver and fact. "Every truly creative individual," writes Schelling, "must create his mythology for himself." Emerson's method is notable for its resistance to this distinction. The New World was for him a Puritan-Romantic text, simultaneously a discovered *figura* of redemptive history and a creation of the symbolic imagination. He undertook a

[4] Emerson, *Works*, ed. E. W. Emerson, 12 vols. (Boston, 1903–1904), I, 150, 364–70, 391; V, 275; XI, 537, 540; Carlyle, *Sartor Resartus*, ed. C. F. Harrold (New York, 1937), p. 220.

figural trial of the center which, proceeding from the thing to the thing signified, fulfilled the self by merging it with the national myth. Insofar as he echoed the European Romantics, he may be said to have posited a double standard for selfhood, American and un-American. Un-Americans he analyzed in static terms, either as indices to the "genius of humanity" (pure intellects like Plato, who transcended time and place), or else as forces of secular history (public leaders like Napoleon, who embodied middle class greed). From this perspective, Emerson had no use for temporal distinctions. "History is a vanishing allegory, and repeats itself to tediousness, a thousand and a million times." Only when he turned to the New World did the past take shape and purpose. Those who "complain of the flatness of American life," he wrote, "have no perception of its destiny. They are not Americans." As a true American, he never wearied of repeating the familiar story—how the continent was "kept in reserve from the intellectual races until they should grow to it," how the Bay planters had undertaken a "holy errand into the wilderness," and how Boston in particular, Winthrop's city on a hill, was "appointed in the destinies of nations to lead . . . civilization." [5]

Emerson's sources for this emergent allegory of history were the writings of the early colonists. He acknowledged them proudly, as a spiritual tribute. Constituting as they did "a bridge between the . . . Hebrew epoch, & our own," the Puritans, he declared, proved that "the Supreme Being exalts the history of this people." His son tells us that he "often spoke of a wish to write the story of Calvinism in New England," in order to com-

---

[5] Whitaker, *Disputation*, tr. W. Fitzgerald (Cambridge, Eng., 1849), p. 407 (my ital.); Schelling, quoted in M. H. Abrams, *Natural Supernaturalism* (New York, 1973), p. 256; Emerson, *Journals and Miscellaneous Notebooks*, ed. W. H. Gilman and others (Cambridge, Mass., 1960–), II, 83; *Works*, XI, 536; XII, 199, 188.

memorate the climactic "triumphs of humanity." Emerson's
project is outlined in his essays from the 1830s through the Civil
War. "The new is only the seed of the old," he wrote in 1841.
"What is this abolition and non-resistance . . . but a continua-
tion of Puritanism. . . ?" In 1863, after non-resistance had
given way to armed conflict, he declared the country to be "in
the midst of a great Revolution, still enacting the sentiment of
the Puritans, and the dreams of young people thirty years ago."
The sacred light that "brought the fathers hither" was guiding
"the visible church of the existing generation" towards an un-
precedented "harvest" of the spirit. It would be irrelevant, in
this context, to point out that the visible American church of
1863 was *not* a fulfillment of the New England Way. Emerson
was obviously speaking of fathers and sons not in any historical
sense, but as aspects of the American idea as this made itself
manifest in his thought. Like Mather's, his filiopietism is a self-
celebrating summons to the future. "GOD WITH THE FA-
THERS, SO WITH US," he declares in his eulogy to Boston,
and then adds: "Let us shame the fathers by superior virtue in
the sons." [6] As *figurae medietatis*, the sons labor to complete the
fathers in a process of exodus, an organic exfoliation of personal
and national divinity, whose essence is the Emersonian-
American self.

Predictably, Emerson found the model of exodus in the
Great Migration. His teleology requires, first, a clear sense of
the past *as* the Old World. "Let the passion for America," he
urges, "extract this tape-worm of Europe from the brains of our

[6] Emerson, *Journals and Notebooks*, II, 72; *Works*, XII, 201; E. W.
Emerson, notes to Emerson, *Works*, I, 437; Emerson, *Works*, XI, 515,
268, 85–86; I, 268–69; *Journals*, eds. E. W. Emerson and W. E. Forbes,
10 vols. (Boston, 1909–14), VI, 52; *Selections*, ed. S. E. Whicher (Boston, 1960), p. 399; *Works*, IX, 217; XII, 210.

countrymen," and with it the stifling veneration of Europe's great men. "To us has been committed by Providence the higher and holier work of forming . . . true and entire men." All others, however high and holy, adumbrate the representative American who is "to prove what the human race can be"—the "exalted manhood" that has been decreed "The Fortune of the Republic." In 1833, after visiting Coleridge, Carlyle, and Wordsworth, Emerson recorded his sense of superiority to all of them and thanked God for bringing him to "the ship that steers westward." Milton may have been an obstacle to Coleridge's self-realization. Emerson thought that Milton—along with Homer, Virgil, Spenser, Swedenborg, Goethe—belonged to an outmoded "feudal school." "Not Shakespeare, not Plato . . . would do." They "call to us affectionately"—"But now all these, and all things else hear the trumpet, and must rush to judgment"; now, "America is a poem in our eyes." [7]

The trumpet that Emerson heard required him—as the second major step in his teleology—to don the robes of a latter-day Nehemiah or John the Baptist. Over and again in his essays and journals, he heralds the New World messiah who will mirror "our incomparable materials." America's "urgent claims on her children . . . yet are all unanswered." "Where are the American writers" who are to solve "the great questions affecting our spiritual nature," where the philosophers and politicians who would adequately express this "country of . . . vast designs and expectations"? Emerson posed these challenges in his early and middle career. In 1868, at the age of sixty-five, after Whitman and

[7] Emerson, *Works*, XI, 535; VI, 145; *Young Emerson Speaks*, ed. A. C. McGiffert, Jr. (Boston, 1938), p. 180; *Journals*, II, 185–86; *Journals and Notebooks*, IV, 79; E. W. Emerson, notes to Emerson, *Works*, I, 451; Roy H. Pearce, *Historicism Once More* (Princeton, 1969), p. 210; Emerson, *Works*, I, 228; III, 38.

Thoreau had in some measure at least answered his call—after Lincoln, Daniel Webster (until 1850), and John Brown had each shown himself a "true representative of this continent," a blend of Revolutionary ardor with the "perfect Puritan faith"—even at sixty-five, Emerson was still seeking the spokesman for the "new era," and still reassuring his audiences that "he shall be found." Since "America is essentially great and *must* produce great men," he explained, "we shall yet have an American genius." [8]

He expressed his faith most fully in "The American Scholar." He calls the essay "one more chapter" in a continuing "biography"—in effect, a prophetic biography of the American self as scholar. It is also, of course, an outline of Emerson's private aspirations. Indeed, several critics have argued that the Scholar is the protagonist of an unwritten *Prelude.* If so, the essay provides a sweeping contrast between American and European Romanticism. Wordsworth hopes to reconstitute in himself all that had been divided, and so must deal with the specifics of his personal and historical condition. Emerson can bypass such considerations because he bears witness to the rising glory of America. Insofar as he projects himself in his hero, he recasts Romantic autobiography into auto-American-biography, reveals himself as harbinger of the nation intended "by all prophecy, by all preparation . . . to fill the postponed expectation of the

[8] Emerson, *Works*, III, 37; *Letters*, ed. R. L. Rusk, 6 vols. (New York, 1939), III, 413; *Early Lectures*, ed. R. E. Spiller and others, 3 vols. (Cambridge, Mass., 1961–72), I, 381, 383, 385; *Works*, III, 38; Henry B. Parkes, "Emerson," in *Emerson*, eds. M. R. Konvitz and S. E. Whicher (Englewood Cliffs, N.J., 1962), p. 132; Emerson, quoted in Michael Cowan, *City of the West* (New Haven, 1967), p. 119, and in Loren Baritz, *City on a Hill* (New York, 1964), p. 259; Emerson, *Works*, XI, 221, 268; VIII, 320; John O. McCormick, "Emerson's Theory of Human Greatness," *New England Quarterly*, XXVI (1953), 313; Emerson, *Works*, I, 370; XI, 537–40.

world." The myth of the primal One Man with which he begins
is a Romantic commonplace. Emerson absorbs the One Man, as
the "exponent of a vaster mind and will," into the Sun of Righteousness advancing across the continental dial. For the European Romantic, the Sun of Righteousness is his own conquering
imagination; *Urzeit* and *Endzeit* embrace in self-discovery: "We
behold as one," cries Los, Blake's archetypal poet, "As One Man
all the Universal Family; and that One Man/ We call Jesus the
Christ." [9]

Blake's concept of Jesus points to the distinction I would
make. It goes without saying that not all European Romantics
asserted a comprehensive selfhood. Many believed they could
achieve that only in infinite approximation; others were content
to await some reintegrated and perfected exemplar of the new
world of the mind. But as their very terms indicate, the ideal
centered upon the self-determining, all-embracing *individual*. In
these terms also, as Meyer Abrams has shown, the Romantics
conceived of historical progression. They believed that humanity was circling "from the One back to the One," in a process of
"self-education" that applied equally to mankind and to each
"reflective" person. Despite their faith in the future, they were
compelled by their commitment to the organic self to identify,
as prophets, with the Jesus of the gospels, the model of the
completed life. For all his commitment to the God within,
Emerson's faith in America compelled him to find his model of
organic selfhood in the coming Son of Man. He wished not to
become Jesus the Christ but to fulfill Him. The Nazarene, according to "The Divinity School Address," serves us as one of
many "noble provocations." He is part of a procession of "divine
bards" that has prepared the way for a "new revelation," by a

[9] Emerson, *Works*, I, 81–82, 110, 114–15; IV, 34; Blake, *Jerusalem*,
II, 38, in *Poetry and Prose*, ed. G. Keynes (New York, 1927), p. 620.

"newborn bard of the Spirit," through whom "America shall introduce a pure religion." From this vantage point Emerson summarized the history of modern theology: "Calvinism rushes to be Unitarianism, and Unitarianism rushes to be pure Theism"; the scriptures contain "immortal sentences; but they have no equal integrity; are fragmentary; are not shown in their order to the intellect. I look for the new Teacher." [10]

The patriotic European Romantic looked in a different direction. The Germans based their mystique of the *Volksgeist* on popular epic and legend; their sense of destiny led them back to the origins of the race, to cultural antiquities. Emerson, like Mather, interpreted the national past through the double focus of prophecies accomplished and prophecies unfolding. In this respect he was perhaps closer to the English Romantics, who resurrected Milton's dream of national election (though they were far enough removed from their Puritan source to center their hopes on the French Revolution). But like Milton they distinguished, ultimately, between personal and national identity—christic and secular selfhood—and accordingly they reenacted the drama of political commitment, disillusionment, and retreat to the kingdom within. By 1837, when Emerson wrote "The American Scholar," their high argument was a revolution of *consciousness*. Blake's Albion symbolizes spiritual wholeness. The "Characters of the great Apocalypse," writes Wordsworth, are "types and symbols of Eternity." When Shelley has Young Atlantis speak the final chorus of *Hellas*—"The world's great age begins anew"—he is saying not that the United States will fulfill history, but that "Freedom belongs to Thought." [11] As a prophetic company, these poets had no country. As English nature

[10] Abrams, *Natural Supernaturalism*, p. 272; Emerson, *Works*, I, 132, 143–46, 149–51; IX, 117, 212.

[11] Wordsworth, *Prelude*, VI.570–71, ed. E. de Selincourt and H.

poets, their allegiance was to the countryside, the specifics of rural life and landscape, the regenerative cycle of the seasons. As citizens, their country, as Milton said after the Restoration, was wherever it is well with one.

Emerson sustained his faith not because the American Revolution was more successful than the French, but because his vision annihilated division. The rhetoric he inherited enabled him to dissolve the differences between history and self—as well as between the different functions of the self (civic, natural, prophetic)—and so to overcome political disenchantment by revealing himself the representative American. Significantly, he conceived his essays on nature, the scholar, and the new religious teacher at the height of what he termed the "emphatic and universal calamity" of the Jacksonian era. The 1828 election of Andrew Jackson was hailed as a spectacular triumph of the young democracy. His re-election in 1832 seemed to Emerson to undermine the very purpose of the Revolution; and the crash of 1837 convinced Emerson that society had "played out its last stake." But with the latter-day theocrats he found that his rhetoric blossomed in adversity. Confronted with a "barbaric" present, he reread the "whole past . . . in its infinite scope," and declared: "Let me begin anew!" His method of self-renewal consisted in investing the meaning of America in himself. God's angel is named freedom, he tells us in a review of the Great Migration. He pronounces his discoveries in thought in the same apocalyptic tone with which he has God say: "Lo! I uncover the land/ Which I hid of old time in the West." To the Romantic notion that "there is no history, only biography," Emerson added two crucial, and crucially related, stipulations: first, that

Darbishire (Oxford, 1959); Carl Woodring, *Politics in English Romantic Poetry* (Cambridge, Mass., 1970), pp. 317–18 (quoting Shelley).

"all biography is autobiography," and second, that "the American idea" concerns neither "caucuses nor congress, neither . . . presidents nor cabinet-ministers, nor . . . such as would make of America another Europe"; it belongs to "the purest minds" only, "and yet it is the only true" idea.[12]

Emerson's conflation of the private with the national ideal characterizes the writings of most of the American Romantics, including the most belligerently anti-nationalistic among them. It is clear, for example, that Thoreau saw America as the golden West of the imagination. It is no less clear that, even at times of active disobedience, he identified the actual movement of the country with the redemptive story of mankind. And it is central to his meaning that we *not* choose between these disparate personal and historical commitments. Dante's new life leads him out of the world's dark forest; Teufelsdröckh's leads him back to the City of Man, but as an alien and a wanderer, circumambulating "the terraqueous Globe." *Sartor Resartus* insists that we distinguish the clothes from the soul, history from the kingdom, modern life from the Everlasting Yea. Thoreau insists upon his clothes, his locale, his life in the woods, as emblems of the American spirit. He does not walk anywhere, but *westward.* His "new country" mode—migrant, "manly," free-enterprising—evokes the frontier dream even as it mocks the Franklinesque Way to Wealth. Mather's Winthrop is an American who has made himself a cornerstone of the New World Jerusalem, and therefore part of the author's figural autobiography. *Walden* is the symbolic autobiography of the self as "the only true America." [13] The bridge between these works is Emerson the prophet, who compensates for political failure by

[12] Emerson, *Journals*, IV, 241; *Works*, IX, 201; V, 286–87; II, 10; VIII, 387.

[13] Carlyle, *Sartor Resartus*, p. 155; Thoreau, *Walden*, in *Walden and Other Writings*, ed. B. Atkinson (New York, 1950), pp. 187, 185.

collapsing history, biography, and autobiography into "the American idea"—by creating himself, figurally, in the image of the New World, even as he internalizes the American experience, symbolically, as a Romantic journey of the soul.

One result of this outlook is the difference between the European and the American cult of genius. Perhaps the most misleading cliché in recent criticism is that our major literature through Emerson is antinomian. The Puritans, we recall, banished Anne Hutchinson because she set her private revelation above the public errand. The controversy foreshadows the fundamentally opposed meanings of greatness in Carlyle and Emerson. Carlyle's hero stands sufficient in himself, a titan born to master the multitude. He is the Frankenstein's monster of left-wing Protestantism, part of a latter-day antinomian brotherhood that includes Shaw's Superman and Ibsen's Master-builder; Nietzsche's Zarathustra, that "terrible teacher of the great contempt"; Byron's exiled saint, whose immortal mind "makes itself/ Requital for its good or evil thoughts." In contrast to all of these, Emerson posed the severely ethical code of the true American. European geniuses, he complained, "have an undisguised . . . contempt for common virtue standing on common principles." Accordingly, he reminded himself in his journals to "beware of Antinomianism," and declared in public that he had undertaken a battle against "mere antinomianism," in the interests of turning society towards the higher laws of chastity, simplicity, spiritual and intellectual awareness. "There was never a country in the world," he felt sure, "which could so easily exhibit this heroism as ours." [14]

[14] Nietzsche, quoted in Stephen Donadio, "Emerson and the Christian Imagination," mss., p. 27; Byron, *Manfred*, III.iv.127–37, in vol. IV of *Works*, ed. E. H. Coleridge, 13 vols. (New York, 1966; reprint of London, 1898–1905 ed.); Emerson, *Works*, IX, 620; *Journals*, IV, 449; *Works*, VII, 119.

Of course, Emerson never denounced antinomianism with
the old Puritan vehemence. Once or twice he spoke of it with a
condescending admiration, as a "vein of folly" that helps the en-
thusiast reach "the people," and often enough we feel a powerful
antinomian impulse in the absolutism of his claims. Nonetheless, his concept of greatness denies the tenets of antinomianism,
in any meaningful sense of the term. More accurately, his teleology redefines his antinomian impulse, somewhat in the manner
of Mather, as the revelation of the American Way. If Emerson's
hero differs from the chauvinist by his Romantic self-reliance,
he differs equally from the Romantic antinomian by his reliance
on a national goal. He speaks not to the fit few, wherever they
are, but to Young America. His natural habitat is not the sublime, anywhere, but the New World. "The land," writes Emerson, "is the appointed remedy for whatever is false and fantastic
in our culture. The land, with its sanative influences, is to repair
the errors of a scholastic and traditional education." This might
be Nehemiah addressing his people in captivity, except that the
land would then evoke the ancient claims of Israel. Or it might
be Luther announcing the doctrine of *sola scriptura*, except that
he would substitute the Bible for nature. Or again, it might be
Wordsworth speaking of his home at Grasmere, except that he
would apply its "sanative influences" to the kingdom within, as
nourishment for the egotistical sublime.

Emerson combines all these themes and transmutes them in
the image of America. His emphasis on nature sustains his myth
of the new holy land; the influences he feels counteract (even as
they complete) the traditions of the Old World; and the regeneration he promises pertains to a "truly Human" nation yet to be
formed. "Greatness appeals to the future," he explains in "Self-
Reliance" and other essays.

It is [therefore] for want of self-culture that the superstition
of Travelling, whose idols are Italy, England, Egypt, re-

tains its fascination for all educated Americans. The force
of character is cumulative. All the foregone days of virtue
work their health into this. They shed a united light on the
advancing actor. The continent we inhabit is to be [our]
physic and food; the native but hidden graces of the landscape [are] intruding a new element into the national mind.
Without looking then to those extraordinary social influences which are now acting in precisely this direction, but
only at what is inevitably doing around us, I think we must
regard the land as the sanative influence, which promises to
disclose new virtues for ages to come. Realize that this
country, the last found, is the great charity of God to the
human race. Accept the place the divine providence has
found for you, the connection of events, transcendent destiny; and [become] guides, redeemers, and benefactors,
obeying the Almighty effort.[15]

Emerson's exhortation to greatness speaks directly to the
paradox of a literature devoted at once to the exaltation of the
individual and the search for a perfect community. Self-reliance
builds upon both these extremes. It is the consummate expression of a culture which places an immense premium on independence while denouncing all forms of eccentricity and elitism.
The denunciation, as Emerson indicates, is less a demand for
conformity than a gesture against antinomianism. Anne Hutchinson's self-reliance, like Wordsworth's, Byron's, Carlyle's, and
Nietzsche's, locates the divine center in the individual. The self-
reliant American is by definition the national benefactor as guide
and prophet. Or prophetess, in the case of Hester Prynne,
Hawthorne's "living sermon" against the "haughty" and "carnal"
Mrs. Hutchinson. To some extent, the "sermon" follows the

[15] Emerson, *Works*, III, 187–88; II, 74, 59–60, 80, 47; I, 391,
364–70, 150; XI, 537, 540. Ellipses deleted.

homiletic tradition of the biblical Esther, *exemplum* of sorrow, duty, and love, and *figura* of the Virgin Mary ("Hester la tres amé/ Ke sauve la genz jugé"). But primarily Hawthorne's argument depends on his heroine's achieving the strength to make herself the *American* Esther. As the "A" she wears expands from "Adulteress" to "Angelic," its significance leads forward from the Puritan "Utopia" to that "brighter period" when the country will fulfill its "high and glorious destiny." More than any other aspect of the novel, it is Hester's intermediate identity that makes *The Scarlet Letter* an American romance. She is neither merely a doomed Romantic Dark Lady at her worst nor wholly a world-redeeming Romantic savior at her best, but a *figura mediatatis*, like Phoebe and Hilda, Endicott and the Gray Champion, a "pledge that New England's sons [and daughters] will vindicate their ancestry." [16]

The prophetic quality of American Romantic heroism expresses the furthest reach of Mather's daring strategy in the *Magnalia*. By comparison, the European great man, for all his superiority to the mass, is sadly restricted. His very self-reliance implies an adversary Other, not only the great precursor but everyone to whom he is superior, everything from which he is alienated—history, the common laws, the representative men and women that constitute social normality. The American self has no such limits. It advances a mode of personal identity intended to embrace both the individual and society, without allowing either for Romantic-antinomian hero-worship or for the

[16] Hawthorne, *Works*, ed. G. L. Lathrop, 15 vols. (Boston, 1882–96), XII, 217–26; Nicholas Baioun, "Prière à la Vierge," quoted in Paul Meyer, "Notice et Extracts du Ms. 8336 de la Bibliothèque de Sir Thomas Philips," *Romania*, XIII (1884), 509; Hawthorne, *The Scarlet Letter*, ed. H. Levin (Boston, 1961), p. 247, and "The Gray Champion," in *Works*, I, 31.

claims of social pluralism. It offers a compensatory *replacement* for (rather than an alternative to) the ugly course of actual events. Hester herself is an inadequate example of this kind of heroism. Because she is part of a larger, complex, highly ironic design, the problems of history assume a weight equal to, if not greater than, the solace she offers. This, at any rate, is the implicit view of those who admire her as an antinomian, and insofar as Hawthorne shared their admiration he upheld the Old World convention, through *Antigone* to *Anna Karenina*, that the great soul reveals itself by confronting social realities and recognizing its limitations.

No doubt *The Scarlet Letter* owes much of its force to the tension between this tragic recognition and the optimism of its New World vision. My point is not to explore the tension, but to note the antithesis. Hester's Emersonian role as prophetess, if I may call it so, militates against the prospect of tragedy because it obliterates contradiction. According to F. O. Matthiessen, the earliest example of Emersonian compensation is the *dictum* that "God is promoted by the worst. Don't despise even the . . . Andrew Jacksons." We can hardly avoid seeing in this formula the strategy by which Emerson, in his seminal essays of the 1830's—sensing his solitude amidst a "wide and wild madness"—proclaimed himself the keeper of the dream. Not by accident his phrases echo those in the *Magnalia's* General Introduction, where Mather announces that "whether New-England may . *live* any where else or no, it must *live* in our History!" Emerson's essays set forth a doctrine of self-reliance, at a crucial post-Revolutionary moment, that lends a new symbolic scope to the Puritan outlook. Geoffrey Hartman has observed that Romantic selfhood took the triadic form of nature, self-consciousness, and imagination. Its issue was not only a victory of the imagination but alternately, and often simultaneously, the "visionary despair" of the "sole self." [17] The Emersonian triad is American nature, the American self, and American destiny, a triple tautology designed to obviate the anxieties both of self-consciousness and of the recalcitrant world.

I am speaking here of the mythic self, of course. All evidence indicates that an enormous private anxiety underlies the affirmation. The Emersonian night of the soul rarely occurs in the open, and never involves the struggle with an external foe. Publicly, the dawn is forever radiant with hope, the enterprise "only at the cock-crowing and the morning star," and the protagonist always young and always "here" (even when he shakes his white locks at the runaway western sun). The struggle takes place in private, in journals, in notebooks, sometimes in letters and *marginalia*. "If I were to write an honest diary," Emerson confided, "what should I say? Alas, that life has shallowness, halfness." And again, more pointedly still: "If . . . the world is not a dualism, is not a bipolar Unity, but is *two*, is Me and It, then is there Alien, the Unknown, and all we have believed & chanted out of our deep instinctive hope is a pretty dream." Stephen Whicher has recorded Emerson's long effort to retain his belief, at the expense of shutting out the tragic vision, which is to say at the expense of self-acceptance. Against the felt dichotomy between Me and It, "the yawning gulf between the ambition of man and his power of performance," against the "double consciousness . . . of the Understanding & of the Soul" which he termed "the worst feature of our biography," Emerson chanted the prophetic self, a "dualism" emptied of two-ness, of

[17] Matthiessen, *American Renaissance* (New York, 1941), p. 318; Emerson, *Journals*, V, 111; Mather, *Magnalia Christi Americana*, ed. T. Robbins, 2 vols. (Hartford, 1853–55), I, 27; Hartman, *Beyond Formalism* (New Haven, 1970), p. 301.

the alien or the unknown—personal and national identity twined in the bipolar unity of auto-American-biography.[18]

The reasons for the suppression of the private life are not far to seek. For Emerson, the evolution of mankind confirms the national mission, American history validates the individual dream, and the autobiographical *exemplum* serves as national prophecy. Granted this correspondence, his Romantic journey outward from subjective to universal stands opposed to the very concept of the incomplete sole self. The personal state, no less than the public, is destiny manifest. "My estimate of America," Emerson confessed, like my "estimate of my mental means and resources, is all or nothing." To despair in oneself is a symbolic gesture of equal magnitude to the affirmation of the dream. It is to declare oneself a *figura* of what we might call the negative apocalypse. The great example here is Melville's Pierre, whose private discovery of ambiguity reverses the national myth embodied in his colonial and Revolutionary sires. "Out of some past Egypt," the narrator begins, "we have come to this New Canaan, and from this New Canaan, we press on to some [ultimate] Circassia." Much later he acknowledges that the Circassia his hero represents is not the New World chiliad, but doomsday. Pierre's deepest despair follows upon the recognition of what for the European Romantic would be a triumphant antinomian epiphany—that the great man stands above the mass, since "all the world does never gregariously advance to Truth, but only here and there some of its individuals do; and by advancing, leave the rest behind." The amplest expression of his despair is Vivia, the protagonist of Pierre's unfinished auto-American-biography—and epitome of Pierre's titanic effort to

[18] Emerson, *Journals*, VI, 200; *Journals and Notebooks*, VII, 200; *Works*, IV, 183; *Journals and Notebooks*, VIII, 10.

cap the "fame-column" of his forebears—who emerges, near the novel's end, as the "American Enceladus," a "foreboding and prophetic" symbol of the void.[19]

One of Pierre-Vivia's precursors is Vivenza, the American utopia described in *Mardi* as "a young Messiah," "promising as the morning." Another is the "Master Genius" Melville hailed in his essay on Hawthorne: the "literary Shiloh of America" who would demonstrate "the supremacy . . . which prophetically awaits us." "We want no American Miltons," Melville declares here, directly after praising Hawthorne for his Calvinism; the very comparison insults any "true American author. . . . Call him an American, and have done; for you cannot say a nobler thing of him." Melville's career is a rapid growth toward this vision, and then a long falling away. *Redburn* and *White-Jacket* transform the journey of the soul into a voyage of the redeemer nation, "homeward-bound" for the millennium; their language is unmistakably Emersonian. The disillusionment that begins in *Mardi* reaches its nadir in *Pierre*, with its profound and savage critique of Transcendentalism. Thereafter the tone varies from Swiftian irony to the modern grotesque, but the original dynamic is transparent throughout, even in the mock-heroic voice of Israel Potter ("prophetically styled Israel by the good Puritans, his parents") who plays a diminished Revolutionary Ishmael to a series of parodic "true Americans"; even in the comic apocalypse of *The Confidence Man*—whose anti-hero, in one of his guises, is Emerson himself—or the bitter detachment of *Clarel:* "To Terminus build Fanes!/ Columbus ended earth's romance:/ No New World to mankind remains." [20]

[19] Emerson, *Works*, VII, 417; Melville, *Pierre*, ed. H. A. Murray (New York, 1949), pp. 37, 8, 482.

[20] Melville, *Mardi*, ed. H. B. Franklin (New York, 1964), p. 412; "Hawthorne and His Mosses," in *The Portable Hawthorne*, ed. M. Cow-

Emerson, too, heard the call of Terminus, "god of bounds," saying "No more!"—as did Thoreau and Whitman. If America is *not* "the Great Western Pioneer whom the nations follow," Thoreau wrote near the end of his life, then "to what end does the world go on . . .?" It was a rhetorical question, of course; and an emendation in an early draft of *Walden* suggests the basis for his persisting optimism. "I could tell a pitiful story respecting myself," he had written, "with a sufficient list of failures, and flow as humbly as the very gutters." His revision, a direct echo of Emerson, became the motto for the entire work: "I do not propose to write an ode to dejection, but to brag as lustily as chanticleer in the morning, standing on his roost, if only to wake my neighbours up." Whitman's mode of compensation is perhaps best seen in his technique of avoidance. No Romantic autobiography, unless we classify "The American Scholar" in that genre, tells us so little about the author as does *Song of Myself*. "Apart from the pulling and hauling stands what I am," Whitman declares; but at the slightest danger of scrutiny he *flees, vanishes, slips away, eludes,* orders us (and presumably himself) to *stand back.* The self which Whitman does sing—which he anatomizes in epic catalogues—belongs to the "divine average," the christic-prophetic *I Am* as the New World: "America isolated yet embodying all, what is it finally, except myself?" [21]

ley (New York, 1967), pp. 413, 419–20; *White-Jacket*, ed. H. Cohen (New York, 1967), pp. 149–50, 302, 399; *Israel Potter*, (New York, 1855), pp. 175, 72, 122, 13–14; *Clarel*, II.250, in vol. XV of *Works*, 16 vols. (New York, 1963; reprint of London, 1922–24 ed.).

[21] Emerson, *Works*, IX, 251; Thoreau, "Walking," in *Walden and Other Writings*, p. 609; "Walden," xerox 1120 of Huntington mss. 924; *Walden* (Boston, 1854), title page and p. 52; Whitman, *Complete Poetry and Selected Prose*, ed. J. E. Miller, Jr. (Boston, 1959), p. 27; Roland Hagenbüchle, "Whitman's Unfinished Quest for an American Identity," *English Literary History*, XL (1973), 469, 450.

When Whitman deleted "myself" from the equation, when he left America on its own, he found it difficult to sustain his optimism. "The people's crudeness, vice, caprices," he admitted, might prove the United States "the most tremendous failure of time." He found it just as difficult to sustain his faith in himself when he deleted "divine" from the average he claimed to express. Considered merely as a poet, he feared, he might turn out to be "the most lamentable of failures . . . in the known history of literature." "All or nothing," Emerson had declared: Whitman, like his Master, found the all in the divine American selfhood he celebrated throughout his career, and never more confidently than during the corruption that followed the Civil War. He denounced the "cancerous" Grant Administration with the righteous fury of a Jeremiah, and, in the same prophetic breath, he salvaged the national ideal by "assuming to himself," as he put it, "all the attributes of his country," en masse. As the American New Man, "acme of things accomplish'd, and . . . encloser of things to be," he could absorb the cheaters and the cheated with equanimity. He has heard the cries of anguish, he tells us, suffered the outrage—and, being "typical of it all," he has beheld also its last result. Proclaiming his good news from atop the "towering selfhood" of "America Herself," he charts the vistas which from eternity "the Almighty had spread before this nation"—the democratic *magnalia Americana*, "dazzling as the sun," to which the present is a morning star. And for our assurance he offers us songs of himself. In his representative life "past and present have interchanged"; his quintessentially American poems give form to "the deepest basic elements and loftiest final meanings of history and man, on which all the superstructures of the future are permanently to rest." [22]

[22] Whitman, reviews in *Walt Whitman*, ed. M. Hindus (New York, 1971), pp. 45, 34–35; *Complete Poetry and Selected Prose*, pp. 456–61, 474,

The superstructures were secured by Emerson. Their foundation was laid in seventeenth-century Massachusetts. Undoubtedly, Mather would have scorned the theology of the young visionary who, a century after his death, took his post as minister of Boston's Second Church. Undoubtedly, too, Whitman differed in important ways from Emerson, as did all the major writers of the American Renaissance. To posit a common design is not to simplify the differences—nor to imply that they are less significant than the similarities—but, on the contrary, to provide a context for discrimination. What is remarkable, from this perspective, is that Emerson's great contemporaries all learned from him to turn the Romantic mode into a vehicle of "the American idea." The qualities that made Emerson the most influential thinker of the period were those which reveal him to be the crucial figure in the continuity of the culture. His achievement lay above all in his synthesis of abiding national themes. At the heart of that synthesis is Emerson the prophet, who in himself vindicates the sons' long labor to complete the fathers. If he succeeded no better than Mather in changing the course of events, he had the prophet's triumph of perpetuating the ideal. And if the facts contradict the teleology he affirmed, which makes the New England Way a foreshadowing, *figura medietatis*, of Transcendentalism, nonetheless he carried the Puritan errand to new heights of eloquence and vision, in a Romantic assertion of the self that fused autobiography and history in the evolving spiritual biography of America.

477, 487, 489, 491, 513, 543, 554. Most of the materials for this essay came from chapter 5 of my forthcoming book, *The Puritan Origins of the American Self* (Yale University Press).

Daniel B. Shea

EMERSON AND THE AMERICAN METAMORPHOSIS

"METAMORPHOSIS IS NATURE." Thus flatly in a Journal entry for 1841 did Emerson declare his matured conviction that the perpetual miracle of nature could best be known in its beautiful changes, indeed could not be fixed in time so as to be known in any other way. His assertion was, of course, organic with its age and place. In its natural supernaturalism, it made botany do the work of theology and testified to the influence of such revelations as Goethe's *Metamorphosis of Plants*. In its prospective air and implicit devotion to process it evoked and emblemized the physical and social transformations of the young Republic. Emerson knew that as the phenomenon of America unfolded, nothing would be final; tendency alone could be assumed; the universal metamorphosis would arise locally as "a field of maize in July," and he exulted in his role as prophet of America's becoming.

It required little conscious reflection for Emerson to catch up the dynamic of American progress in an organic metaphor. He needed only to allow "the spirit of the hour to pass unobstructed through [his] mind," as he said of Shakespeare. But in 1841, with the publication of the *Essays: First Series*, he had to be fully conscious of the metamorphic quality of his own career. In the decade from 1826 to 1836 he had found a vocation, lost it, and then recovered it again in another shape. The junior pastor of the Second Church of Boston had become the author of *Nature*, effecting a version of the American Metamorphosis more striking than most for its congruence of biographical act and literary word. In his own case he had recapitulated the Puritan's regeneration,[1] the egocentric intentionality of Franklin's rise to a comely and serviceable estate, and Crèvecoeur's narrative of the American as new man—the "American resurrection," D. H. Lawrence called it in recounting the Farmer's parable of bees revived out of the belly of a king-bird.

The term *metamorphosis* and the range of subjects associated with its use appear throughout Emerson's work, shifting in import as his ideas developed and contended against each other. These developments are familiar, and a single term, even one so central as metamorphosis, serves only to supply an additional index to them. But in addition to the metamorphoses of the man and the variations in theme signalled by this most intriguing of his metaphors, there is the metamorphic quality of the writing itself. Transmuted experience was Emerson's ideal of form, and he deserves to be tested by his own criterion. If, following Stephen Whicher's suggestion, we read Emerson—both the life in the work and the life of the work—as dream or romance, his writing becomes fully integrated with other characteristic products of the American imagination. Whicher himself began to read Emerson in this way. Jonathan Bishop has done so with a considerable advance in formal and verbal sensitivity. And more

---

[1] The assertion of one seventeenth-century sermon could be duplicated in dozens of others: "But you must be transformed (or metamorphosed) by the renewing of your heart and life; the old frame must be dissolved and a new one acquired." This anonymous sermon is quoted in a stimulating study of the "metamorphic aesthetic" of early New England gravestones, Dickran and Ann Tashjian, *Memorials for Children of Change* (Middletown, Conn., 1974), p. 18.

recently, Lawrence Buell has proposed a literary Emerson who brings to fruit the imaginative possibilities inherent in the Puritan and Unitarian traditions.[2] What remains to be attempted, I believe, when the Belknap editors have completed their work, is a thorough genetic study of Emerson the writer, a critical history of the extended autobiographical prose-poem which he created.

For Emerson is the crucial figure in a tradition that has helped identify American literature, the celebration and testing of the proposition that "men are convertible"—an institutionalized article of faith to the Puritans but one that has been vexed by second thoughts ever since. By raising again the question of grace, Emerson gave extended life to the seventeenth-century spiritual autobiography. By precept and example he challenged the American writer to deliver up out of his experience a transformed language and imaginative structures more nearly organic with an American conception of man as endlessly capable of regeneration. Such a challenge ought not to yield the novel's standard progression, in which a central character moves upward through long-established levels of society, or in which the character, interacting with a society both alluring and problematic, comes to rest in increased self-understanding. The kind of becoming suggested in the symbol of the transparent eyeball is metamorphic, not simply a change of status but a change of state; the attainment of a newly-given self, not simply the regaining of identity through recognition. Without Ovid's recourse to the gods, the American writer after Emerson is challenged to induce belief that something extrinsic to the character has, in a transforming moment, become intrinsic to him. Something apparently not in the system of the protagonist's growth,

[2] *Literary Transcendentalism: Style and Vision in the American Renaissance* (Ithaca, 1973).

but deriving from his natural environment, perhaps from the American spirit of place, invades and transforms the self. From such a point of view, American books may well appear as so many varieties of religious experience and William James a better guide to them than the literary historian.

In its earliest literary manifestations, in Thoreau and Whitman for instance, the American Metamorphosis has the dignity of a fable whose adequacy has been tested in primary experience. Reappearing in such works as *Go Tell It on the Mountain* and *The Adventures of Augie March*, it has the continued authenticity of a fiction durable enough to be true to new kinds of fact. But the idea of metamorphosis has other connotations, frequently traced to Emerson. It suggests a blithe belief in indefinite and automatic progress; it smacks of a Shazam mentality and an inane coveting of psychic upward mobility; it pants for a new series of changes without having assimilated the last. In reaction, American literature has gained plausibility through works that reflect ironically upon the metamorphosis, imitating the shape of belief in order to correct or dissolve it. One thinks of *Wieland*, *A Connecticut Yankee in King Arthur's Court*, *The Red Badge of Courage*, *Sister Carrie*.

To estimate Emerson's culpability in these matters, even properly to credit him with calling forth opposition, would require an elaborate inquiry into historical cause and effect. Another approach through which initially to view Emerson and metamorphosis would be to step out of American literature entirely, setting the Emersonian contours against those of a literary text, *The Metamorphosis* of Kafka, which owes nothing to Concord. To the polarizing mind, a delicious sense of contrast between absolutes lurks here in the zenith and nadir of metamorphic possibilities. Emerson, fully escaped from chrysalis, is all wings and ascension. Kafka's monstrous dung-beetle renders our fall into fixity, enclosure, and pathetic, belly-up vulnerability. For the comparatist of ironic inclination, the one scene lacking in Kafka would have an American visitor slipping a copy of "Self-Reliance" under Gregor Samsa's bedroom door.

Like the transparent eyeball, Kafka's symbol is, for its hero, autobiographical and expressive, but in a reflexive way. It is as if the loathsome beetle had been created out of the eyes of Gregor's parents and sales-manager. Or to put it another way, Gregor becomes what he believes others see in him once they have pierced the regularity of his habits and his apparent filial devotion to lay bare the surreptitious sexual and imaginative life within. His transformation anticipates in time, then creates in fact, their sickened disgust at this discovery. Gregor becomes the victim of his imagined transparency and the prisoner of his self-consciousness. His self-loathing is suicidal both in tendency and result.

In his chaste and tempered way, Emerson may have been testifying to a comparable kind of awareness when in his first sermon he asked his congregation "whether the idea that other beings can read his thoughts, has not appeared so natural and probable," that a man will sometimes suppress "thoughts that seemed too daring or indecent, for any unknown beholders to be trusted with." Emerson's horrible secret, daring but never indecent, was in Stephen Whicher's phrase, "the dream of greatness." "Shall I embroil my short life with a vain desire of perpetuating its memory when I am dead & gone in this dirty planet?," he asks himself at 21, and goes on to disparage his "best boast that I am the citizen of a far country far removed from the low influence of earth & sea, of time & change. . . ." So well schooled does he become in viewing himself through the eyes of others that he can recite their condemnations, speak their part:

> . . . it is wholly a fanciful scheme, such as boys all have in
> their turn and all sound minds outgrow—. . .man is born
> by the side of his father, and *therefore* should remain a social
> being. . . . So 'twere better you did not set your judgment
> against the whole world's, and so ruin a promising youth
> by falling into disesteem & opprobrium.

This is very nearly the voice of Gregor's father, who finally
wins the Oedipal struggle, waxing as his son wanes and dealing
a mortal blow by hurling the apples of guilt into the beetle's
back. Though not threatened directly by paternal authority,
Emerson knew its weight in the tradition of the New England
ministry to which his father belonged and could guess sympa-
thetically how well his contemporaries were carrying their burden. "At times," he thought, "the land smells with suicide.
Young men have no hope." The same young men, "of the fairest
promise," reappear in *The American Scholar* to "turn drudges, or
die of disgust, some of them suicides." They have arrived in a
world in which men "are bugs, are spawn. . . ." So there are
grounds for thinking that the young Emerson, obscene in his
fantasy of greatness and vulnerable to definition by the world's
eye, might after all have read Kafka with comprehension. He
was prepared, certainly, to understand the vehicle of nightmare.
If one takes beasts to be the dreams of nature, he surmised, then
by reversal, our dreams, with their "unsurprised assent to the
monstrous," hint at the imprisoned consciousness of beasts
whom we may think of as "metamorphosed men." The "strange
melancholy" of a degraded metamorphosis lingers equally in the
glances of animals or men trapped in a debased condition. Only
the impossibility of seeing his condition from the outside pre-
vents the beast, or the man thus symbolized, from self-destruc-
tion. Ovid is no fiction, Emerson asserts, in a formula no less
applicable to Kafka, for his "fables are our own thoughts carried
out."

I

We know now that Emerson's ambitious soul was delivered from its imprisoned state, but in the early journals both the outcome and the value of the fable are in doubt. For the young Emerson, greatness and grace are nearly indistinguishable. The reader understands that the son of a minister will pray, but that he should implore heaven to avert from him an insignificant fate, explaining, "I need excitement," suggests a piety that bears watching. Like the keeper of a Puritan diary, this latter-day casuist of the soul's deliverance warns his more sanguine self that it must never mistake the hope for the reality, though hope may be a promising token, then pounces upon his deadliest sin—that languishing in a "dream of honour"—which could finally prevent his achieving it. A succession of journal passages brightened by the rubric GREATNESS, in capital letters, is perhaps balanced by others that describe the grandeur of virtue, but virtue comes to seem an ambition like any other.

The first Emerson was an Arminian. He would earn his grace. Those who serve their fellow men, he decides, procure themselves "a longer memory in this world, (& perchance in worlds beyond,). . . ." With perfect deliberateness, Emerson casts up his weaknesses and strengths and decides that the formality and love of eloquence he has inherited from his "sire" permit him a reasonable expectation of thriving in Divinity. But his vocation is less a call than a cry in the dark. The well-known passage in which Emerson binds himself to the ministry is preceded by the despairing admission, "It may be I shall write *dupe* a long time to come. . . ." By taking the form to himself he hopes to engender the reality. In a confusion no Puritan would have made, he sees conversion as an effect of profession: "My trust is my profession shall be my regeneration of mind, manners, inward & outward estate. . . ." In the matter of "extraor-

dinary conversions," Emerson had good reason for later asserting that "the rod of this metamorphosis, God holds in his own
hand. . . ."

For all his sensitivity to native religious traditions, Emerson
chose to ignore the Puritans' accumulated experience of humilia-
tion and brokenness as the necessary antecedents of grace. Even
after his own devastation in the death of his first wife, Ellen, he
would not preach the doctrine, though he exemplified it. It is
generally acknowledged that the death of Ellen turned Emerson
around—converted him one may say—so that he fronted on
eternity. The image of an ideal self loosed itself from time and
the social institution of marriage, for as both woman and oc-
casional poetess, Ellen qualified twice over for the term *angel*,
which Emerson used to describe her. The nineteenth century,
prescient as always, knew its Jung. When Emerson observed in
the first summer of his marriage, "Every man contemplates an
angel in his future self," he identified Ellen and *anima* so closely
that at her death his Platonic conception of himself was able to
effect its escape from the confining role in which it had been
housed. Had he not been able to believe that Ellen was "nowhere & yet everywhere," Emerson confessed in verse, "I
would bury my ambition / The hope & action of my sovereign
soul. . . ."

A full year before he proposed changes in the administration of the Lord's Supper to a committee of the Second Church,
but only four months after Ellen's death, Emerson was proclaiming his rebirth: "You are free to follow the natural constitution of your mind & the Universe." A dead skin was being
sloughed, a cocoon abandoned. Whatever else may have moved
Emerson, it was with an uncanny sense of the symbolic that he
shortly afterward went to Roxbury to open Ellen's coffin, as if
to view at the same time the remains of his corpse-cold Uni-

tarianism. "The stark and stiffened corpse is the emblem of the past," he would tell a lecture audience. Even to the more retrospective author of "Society and Solitude," memory is the Medusa, transforming what should be a perpetually seminal life into stone. Emerson's cryptic jotting, "Today I found in Roxbury the Saxifrage Vernalis," requires William Carlos Williams' "A Sort of a Song" for its translation: "Saxifrage is my flower that splits / the rocks."

Metamorphosis implies that in a latter form of growth there is always something of previous stages; we should inspect the prince closely for warts. The metamorphosis of experience in art, however, requires that the prosaic autobiography remain hidden. If the reader can say, "this is Andrew and that is Rachel. . . . It is a caterpillar with wings, and not yet a butterfly." Perhaps the clearest demonstration of Emerson's principle occurs in the concluding paragraphs of "Compensation" in which the speaker hints at the kind of transforming revolution in which "angels go . . . that archangels may come in." His experience finally takes the shape of a dichotomous metaphor. Against the image of a complacently domesticated flower "with no room for its roots and too much sunshine for its head," stands another, the emblem of Emerson's personal metamorphosis and achieved vocation, "the banian of the forest, yielding shade and fruit to wide neighborhoods of men." What is below the earth nourishes what is above it, and the artist perhaps knows this best of all. Defining the poet, Emerson acknowledges: "we study to utter our painful secret. The man is only half himself, the other half is his expression." The working of internal and external pressures against each other results in a form which is neither wholly personal nor strictly autonomous. Even the most apparently impersonal of Emerson's symbols, the central symbol of *Nature,* has its affinities with his comment on love: "we became all eye when one was present, and all memory when one was gone." Emerson rejects history to the same extent and with as much success as metamorphosis rejects previous forms. In the essay on "History" Emerson cites the transformations of Io from woman to cow to woman and notes that her final beauty was enhanced by what remained of her "lunar horns." Certainly he did not, as Quentin Anderson has argued, deny "a history of successive and transcendent changes in the psyche." [3] That was precisely the meaning of his own metamorphosis.

II

Confirmed by experience, the notion of metamorphosis served Emerson well through the distinctive stages of his development. His incapacity for discursive logic and the tendency of his mind to convert the Many into One and back again regularly created the need for a metaphor both Protean in substance and prolific in implication. At various times he employs metamorphosis to mean: the soul's awakening; the perpetual miracle of nature; the leap of natural fact into spiritual fact as symbol or metaphor; simple process; process as becoming and amelioration; the dynamic of nature by which spiritual law is visibly incarnated; and, in the social order, the decay of institutions and their replacement by increasingly humane and therefore divine systems of organization.

None of these implications is promised in Emerson's first, fastidious references to a pagan invention. In 1822 his Puritan disdain for fiction as an artful flourishing of untruth led him to speak condescendingly of fables as primitive devices for the re-

[3] *The Imperial Self* (New York, 1971), p. 19.

lief of human misery—metamorphosis, particularly, striking "the ear of taste" as offensive. If there is any moral in Ovid, it is "Trust not the Passions." All those tumblings backward into beast in "strange metamorphosis" only illustrate the sudden passage of the sinner from saving inhibition to a delight in "enormities." But by 1840, when he read in Rabelais about a Dominican friar who had published a spiritualization of *The Metamorphoses*, Emerson had accomplished the task for himself.

Or almost by himself. He had a good deal of help from Goethe's *Metamorphosis of Plants*, whose theory of the ur-plant Emerson would later refer to as "the leading idea of modern botany." Still elated by the experience in the Jardin des Plantes which suggested occult sympathies between man and nature and set him looking for the clue to their joint classification, Emerson responded immediately to Goethe's description of "the Arch plant, which, being known would give not only all actual but all possible vegetable forms." Yet in an 1836 lecture on the "Humanity of Science," just after he had hailed again Goethe's "prophetic vision" of metamorphosis, Emerson cited Lamarck's comparable attempt to find a monad of organic life as an example of the mind's impatience "in the presence of a multitude of facts. . . ." The monad, to which he objects, and the ur-plant, which he accepts, seem alternative versions of the same notion of ultimate form. The distinction Emerson observes, however, is that between the research of the scientist and the quest of the poet. While deriving from botanical study, the ur-plant strikes Emerson as a poetic hypothesis constantly being verified by impressions of unity arising out of multiplicity. Then, too, the monad is static. Goethe's ur-plant is defined in its changes of form, arising, Emerson says in figurative apostrophe, out of the "eye or germinative point," and moving through all the variations—radicle, stamen, pistil, petal, bract, sepal, seed—of the

essential leaf. Emerson had no mental itch to work out a philosophical consistency between the One and the Many, but as
poet and rhetorician he badly needed a way of talking about two
truths of perception at once. Metamorphosis, the observable
process in nature by which something changes while maintain-
ing its identity, was that way of talking.

Goethe, Pythagoras, and Swedenborg, whose names are
linked in the 1834 Journal passage I have been dwelling on, are
all adherents of what Emerson called somewhat Germanically,
"the Identity-Philosophy." But other more philosophically re-
spectable names would have met the same test. The real kinship
among these figures derives from their contributing a basis of literal belief (whether in the metamorphosis of plants, or metempsychosis, or the doctrine of "affections clothed") to Emerson's
metaphoric imagination; or, in presenting him with symbolic
versions of the ongoing metamorphosis of spirit into nature in
which Emerson himself believed. The proposition, like metaphor itself, is symbiotic.

In either case, metamorphosis makes an unstated unity
among these three names. In Ovid's *Metamorphoses*, the 400 lines
in which Pythagoras explains to Numa the transmigration of
souls supply a canopy of theme for individual fables of transformation. Swedenborg's doctrine of "affections clothed" perceives
the divine efflux taking on form through human thought and
feeling, which in turn fashion the world's circumstances to correspond precisely with that form. Metamorphosis occurs when
feelings mix with matter. "The moment we indulge our affections," Emerson tells himself, "the earth is metamorphosed:
there is no winter and no night: all tragedies, all ennuis vanish;—all duties even. . . ." The complete Journal passage from
which this remark comes is yet another revery on Ellen and was
later trimmed for inclusion in "Friendship." Most readers,

though, will be reminded of the conclusion of *Nature*, with its promise that an influx of spirit, working through man, will effect the disappearance of the disagreeable. This assertion, and others like it in the section called 'Prospects," are rightly taken to demonstrate the combined influence on Emerson of Swedenborg and Neo-Platonic philosophy. But it is no less true to say that the metaphor of metamorphosis so thoroughly informs Emerson's prose in the conclusion of *Nature* that it solves problems for him even when only implicitly present.

Entering the poet's world as revelation, metaphor becomes in use a problem-solving device. Emerson could afford to be only a half-hearted believer in the hypothesis of Idealism because his allegiance to metaphor, and to that of metamorphosis in particular, gave him a more profound basis for knowing that things were transformed ideas and that affective ideas altered the shape of matter. Against the philosophical conundrums of spirit and matter, subject and object, One and Many, a metaphor is his sufficient reply. Each term of a pair proceeds from the vision of one eye only. In experience they are always being transformed into one another:

> The rushing metamorphosis
> Dissolving all that fixture is
> Melts things that be to things that seem,
> And solid nature to a dream.
>
> (*Woodnotes II*)

This is not to say that the notion of metamorphosis shows no signs of stress, since it must do its work in the area between powerful polarities and is wedded in development to changes taking place within Emerson himself. But it proved sufficiently adaptable to survive the transitional period Stephen Whicher first described in which faith in the transcendent self was replaced by trust in the ultimately benevolent tendency of natural processes. The first faith gives a sense of what the soul has always been and may, in a surge of instinct, repossess; the second is more patient and can wait through eons of evolution for the world spirit to complete its ascending journey. Discovering his myths in conflict, Emerson could take heart from the example of Ovid, who began his poem with mankind falling away from an Age of Gold, yet brought it to a close with the apotheosis of Julius Caesar and implicitly of the Roman state. Carl Strauch, working out the terms of Emerson's accommodation between his early poetical belief in Neo-Platonic emanation and his later more naturalistic confidence in biological evolution, suggests that "it is probably because Emerson 'believed in' emanation that he 'believed in' evolution." [4] Strauch's perception might be altered without distortion to read: because Emerson "believed in" metamorphosis, he continued to believe.

In the death of his son Waldo, both his personal and cosmic senses of ameliorative process were severely challenged. The question put to the father's grief in the poem "Threnody" is, which will he surrender, his son or his assent to process. If it were in his power would he make the choice that halts the flow, transfixes life, and thereby negates it? In Emerson, such a choice is not in fact outside the power of the mind. Like the body's talent for death, vision has the capacity for blindness, for converting the earth into tomb and relic. The burden of tabulating the works of metamorphosis in a private ledger is enormous: does one count births or deaths, fingers or cracks; is it she loves me, or she loves me not? The arbitrariness of extrapolating from a merely personal tally finally grew clear to Emerson.

The logic of Emerson's response to his second humbling is

[4] "Emerson's Sacred Science," *PMLA*, 73 (Jan. 1958), p. 238.

not flawless. I mean only to suggest that a resilient metaphor provided him with an instrument for order—in Emily Dickinson's phrase, "a plank in reason," which could bear weight. "Everyone has bitterness in his chosen thing," says a Saul Bellow character, and because metamorphosis was one of the ways Emerson spoke about his chosen thing it helped give form to the potentially destructive outcroppings of his skeptical period, a time in which his own premises turned on him threateningly.

III

The painful turn in Emerson's monologic drama is the way in which the speaker's entrapment makes ironic continuity with his earlier plot for freedom. In "Experience," the metamorphosis of object into subject continues as before, but with altered valence because Intellect now stands outside the process and coldly watches the affections blending experience according to their own quaint recipe. Spirit continues to put forth its own house, but no longer as freeholder; in "Fate," "the house confines the spirit," and other renderings of the metamorphosis of affections into circumstances suggest a deep revulsion at the stink of self: "the slug sweats out its slimy house on the pear-leaf, and the wooly aphides on the apple perspire their own bed. . . ." The miraculous sloughing of inefficacious selves has stopped. "People seem sheathed in their own tough organizations." The flow of process that had once seemed perpetual miracle now shows only its surface and hurries the mind from illusion to illusion.

As these essays finally right themselves, certain phrases make one wish the metamorphosis could run backwards. The reader could then leave behind the exhortation "up again, old heart!," leave unfinished the building of altars to a Beautiful Necessity, and savor at the end the hovering of epistemological darkness in the boughs of the fir-tree and the sharp devaluations of a "pistareen-Providence." The total form of these essays, however, redeems individual expressions and embodies the principle by which their dramas of contradiction have been resolved. To state such a principle is never a finished task, and in seeking a new vocabulary there is no need to relinquish others—the twice-bisected line, the angle of vision, the ascending spiral— that have illuminated Emerson's most challenging work. The language of dialectic—Emerson's throwing his weight now on one horse, now another; his two boys, matter and spirit, jostling each other on the curbstone—has always accorded well with the facts of our reading experience.

And yet Emerson said, "Life is not dialectics," by which he meant that against recalcitrant experience, a theory is an old mare. The great essays "Experience" and "Fate" accomplish something more than the paper victory of dialectical opposition and synthesis. They do not eke out their sublimities by a "theatrical trick," as Emerson said of the heavens created by candlelight on the roof of a crystal-specked cave. Whatever of Puritanism remained alive in Emerson told him that the Word is still-born when not delivered out of the preacher's own experience. What he had experienced was not the dialectic of intellect, but of nature, a succession of increasingly prolonged periods of prosaic calendar time and increasingly rare infusions of revelatory light. Whether from a memory of Goethe or directly now from his own increasingly refined awareness of internal and external process, Emerson was discovering that metamorphosis goes forward in two phases—one progressive, the other regressive.

In the botanical terms used by Goethe, progressive metamorphosis takes place in successive stages from seed to fruit; regressive metamorphosis occurs when the form of the leaf contracts itself into the sexual organs of stamen and pistil and their protective petals and sepals.[5] Apparently weakened by its retreat within the calyx, the plant is in fact undergoing a new creation. In his poem, "The Metamorphosis of Plants," Goethe describes nature "less abundantly yielding the sap, contracting the vessels," then suddenly unfolding in "brilliant-hued coronals . . . in glory still nobler and fuller. . . ." What Goethe calls the *Steigerung*, the heightening or ascension, can take place only as the result of interplay between these two movements, an aspiring and a contractive principle.

Regressive metamorphosis is the state in which Emerson finds himself at the beginning of "Experience," or, in the dramatic terms appropriate to that essay, it is the role he takes on. Here and in "Fate" the surest sign of change in Emerson is the retrenchment in meanings associated with metamorphosis, while the surest sign of continuity is the total metamorphic form of the essays. The equationary formulas of "Compensation," with its figures from business and arithmetic, have been left behind for more adequate ways of dramatizing his spiritual autobiography. Speaking in a first-person plural that generalizes his sense of depleted energies, Emerson describes a weight of routine so oppressive "that the pith of each man's genius contracts itself to a very few hours." The dramatic issue in suspense is whether this contraction will close off perception entirely. The speaker

[5] Goethe's influence on Emerson is well documented, but students of Emerson can learn much from a richly suggestive study of *Faust* which does not mention Emerson at all. My reading of Emerson at this point is indebted to Peter Salm's aesthetic applications of the botanical metaphor in *The Poem as Plant* (Cleveland, 1971). Goethe's poem, "The Metamorphosis of Plants" is readily available in English translation, but it is the prose treatise, *Versuch die Metamorphose der Pflanzen zu erklären*, to which Emerson refers. For a translation see *Chronica Botanica*, 10 (1946), pp. 63–115, introduction and translation by Agnes Arber.

who can call the death of his son a merely caducous process, leaving no scar, evidently views metamorphosis as gradual extinction. Sighting ahead, he takes a "grim satisfaction" in the reality of his own death, which the process guarantees.

The contracting of vision almost into darkness comprises the opening strophe of the essay. In it, the essayist becomes a dramatic event by diminishing himself into a kind of "subperson," and his preachments, similarly contracted, never exceed in boldness the advice of one drowning man to another: go with the current; "go about your business"; treat the men and women "as if they were real"; settle for the goods "on the highway." To elevate himself above the extinguishing process and to effect a turn in the drama, Emerson raises his voice into the first-person singular: "If I have described life as a flux of moods, I must now add. . . ." As writer, he is capable of commanding the metamorphosis and of ordaining its tendency by keeping "the mighty Ideal" journeying ahead. So we should not be dismayed when the essay suffers a second regression. The Fall of Man, retold as a fable of solipsism, follows upon and appears to crush a premature flowering, the melodramatic outburst "Onward and ónward!" Recovery takes place, however, and within briefer compass than that of the initial movement, when the speaker catches sight of a god among the "bleak rocks" toward which he is headed. The first prolonged alternation between regressive and progressive metamorphosis repeats itself in quickened succession to bring about a rebirth of "the world I think." The essay, as the man, "lives by pulses," reveals that its "chemical and ethereal agents are undulatory and alternate," and by increasingly vigorous self-recoveries "possesses its axis more firmly." In Whitman, of course, these fits and pulses would be orgasmic, just as in Goethe the two kinds of metamorphosis "lovingly blend into one" under the governance of Eros. By contrast, Emerson's venture into metamorphic form may appear a New England version of parthenogenesis, at most only schematically sexual, like the relation between Power and Form. Guiltless of seed, Ellen bears a different progeny from Goethe's Helen.

The speaker in "Fate" is not the frequently unreliable narrator of "Experience." Because in *The Conduct of Life* Emerson speaks to the issue "How shall I live?," he is always explicit, even in his rejections. The precarious dramatic sense of ultimate values being tested is no less sharp, however, and metamorphosis, I believe, is again the medium of their endurance. Goethe's archetypal leaf has been replaced by ovarian vessicles, which, developing in darkness, become animals, in light, plants. Internal force must surrender the final decision on form to the shaping power of environment. At any given moment in nature the circumstance appears tyrannous and its limitations absolute; and in any given utterance of the essay—"Ask the digger in the ditch to explain Newton's laws," for example—nature's *fiat* is proclaimed with relief at being able to state observable fact without sentiment.

But both nature and essay are in process. Limitation cultivates expansion. "Fate involves the melioration" because its limiting pressures call forth redoubled power. And once the writer has limited his options, they begin to proliferate. It is like Vishnu following Maya "through all her ascending changes"; moving upward, the antagonisms between counter-forces become increasingly refined. Emerson had always figured development organically, but now his earlier metaphors—the melon's expansion, the oak from the acorn, the prodigious growth of the mustard seed—seem banal, predictable, and unchallenged, presumptuous of grace and good weather. The double-consciousness, which is Intellect's version of the two-fold metamorphosis, sustains a creative antagonism in "Fate" that pits higher and lower vocabularies against each other and that converts any image—the steam locomotive, a piece of mosaic, "reluctant granite"—to higher purpose. Now, "any chip or pebble will bud and shoot out winged feet and serve him for a horse." The metaphor is not so much mixed as metamorphic; mineral becomes vegetable becomes animal.

In these two essays, for the sake of which one is willing to forgive acres of his optimism, Emerson has retained his identity as nature's advocate while obeying the necessity to change so as to live. Into his final stages metamorphosis brings forward something of his beginnings. His saving rediscovery of the relation between brokenness and grace makes him more the Puritan than when he first left the pulpit. "Nature will not spare the smallest leaf of laurel. All writing comes by the grace of God, and all doing and having." Grace no longer appears spontaneously generated, but contingent. Self and society continue to be distinguished, but each has its own perquisites, and their relation is no longer inimical. Imperial self not only grants the power of lordly environment, but does it a kind of homage. Love, poverty, war, religion, trade, art, science—all are acknowledged as helping to effect the metamorphosis: their "loud taps on the tough chrysalis can break its walls and let the new creature emerge erect and free. . . ." This, we know, is where Emerson comes out. The author of *The Conduct of Life* himself hardens into acquiescent form as original life passes out of him and, one imagines, into the 1860 edition of *Leaves of Grass*.

IV

In the end it was clear to Emerson that he could only have become what he was, but the problem of vocation had not ended in 1832, or with the publication of *Nature*, because its basis in Emerson's character had not disappeared. The conflict which Henry Nash Smith observed in first defining Emerson's dilemma, that between a desire for active reform and a tendency toward passive contemplation, simply assumes different forms after its first resolution in favor of a literary career. The scene of the conflict moves within literature itself. In "The American Scholar," thought and action exist in a mutually energizing relationship, but what kind of action, after all, was an essay or a lecture or a poem? Perhaps out of his life-long fascination with Napoleon, Emerson liked to think of the lecturer's eloquence as a kind of conquest, a well-intentioned despotism "taking sovereign possession of the audience." In the period of his ascendant ego, rhetoric was the magnanimous act of extending the periphery of his own spiritual triumph. He would convert his audiences by immersing them in his own vision, leading them on by hyperbole while creating a sense that there remained, still, a little beyond.

But when vision dimmed, two things were likely to happen. Rhetoric could become a personal tactic for survival, while continuing to act for the common good, as in "Experience" and "Fate." Or it could be abandoned altogether, solipsism burning its bridge to other selves. The latter possibility had always been implicit in Emerson's introversion, glaringly so in the title he chose for his first private writing. "I love my Wideworld," he said, distinguishing it from ours. At their most communicative, his essays had always shown a certain amount of rhetorical disdain. They are often the angels he describes in "Intellect"—"so enamored of the language that is spoken in heaven" that they speak their own dialect "whether there be any who understand it or not." The Emersonian metamorphosis is at a crucial stage when a "private fruit" may be sufficient.

Hence the transitional importance to Emerson, in the early 1840's, of the figure of the poet. More private in vision than either the essayist or the lecturer, he nevertheless acts, words being actions and actions "a kind of words." The maker of "Uriel" does not follow Uriel into his cloud, leaving nature to vindicate him. Only the vibrations of Emerson's so inclining can be felt in the 1844 essay on "The Poet," stilled by its major themes. The death of his son in 1842 had driven Emerson into poetry as a refuge; the poet is said to leave behind the funereal tolling of the world's time for the exclusive company of the muse. In retreat, Emerson rethought the lecture on the poet he had been delivering during the winter of his son's death, with the result that the second version contains an unusually large increment of fresh writing. The poet's act is one of liberation, and the essay "Experience," with which "The Poet" is linked by sequence and by the phrase "dream delivers us to dream," shows us what the poet can liberate us from: meaningless flux and inundating change. As Emerson's richest development of the theme of metamorphosis, the essay on the poet is a necessary prelude to the unsettling data of "Experience."

The metamorphosis is one, but in poetry its manifestations are three and inter-related. The poet sees the world under glass, Emerson says. Undistracted by surface illusion, he pierces through to the vital and "incessant metamorphosis" beneath. The poet's catching sight of the life behind appearances and his speaking what he sees are two phases of the same process. Properly speaking, the fashioned poem "is not art, but a second nature, grown out of the first, as a leaf out of a tree." Poetic speech is a sacrament in which nature, working through the poet, "baptises herself; and this through the metamorphosis again." The poem is captured grace, distilled from the natural process of experience, and as such it detaches from the poet a deathless "new self" not plagued by the coming and going of light in diurnal experience. For the reader, too, poetry is conversion. The transforming grace inherent in the poem enters us through our participating imagination, exciting joy, and bestowing the "new sense" of a world within the world, or rather a "nest of worlds; for the metamorphosis once seen, we divine that it does not stop."

A covenant made in the imagination, poetry offered an assurance of salvation. Its promise of allowing participation in nature's essential process, so that one returned at any time to what was out of time, was a constant in Emerson's experience of the relation between life and art. Paradoxically, this assurance enabled Emerson to pass through the role of poet and to undergo the final transformation of his literary career. To enjoy the private fruit of poetry might sustain the soul, but it was not the kind of fruitfulness demanded by the prudential, the incarnational Emerson. In the end, he became what he always was; his man speaking to other men is simply a writer. *Representative Men*, which is Emerson's last rehearsal of all the roles available to him, allots its final and decisive chapter to Goethe, the writer, rather than to Shakespeare, the poet. While its subject matter is familiar, *Representative Men* takes on renewed interest when seen as a meditative space within which Emerson acts out in consummate fashion his perennial drama of vocation and when it is understood to rest on that "necessary and autobiographic basis" without which, he said, our reading of any book would be a waste of time.

His representative men are Emerson's final metamorphoses, even to the point of meriting the secondary sense, in German, of Kafka's *Die Verwandlung*—the changing of scenes on a theater stage. But the sequence of changes does not bring us as it did in 1836 from the level of commodity upward to the level of spirit.

Through Plato and Swedenborg, spirit has its say early, and we then move in the direction of Napoleon, the materialistic hero, whose life rather than Goethe's would have concluded the volume according to several of Emerson's early projections. Vaporous spiritualism and mere literariness inspire disgust as readily as arrogant materialism: "Plato is weak inasmuch as he is literary," Emerson had said. "Shakespeare is not literary, but the strong earth itself." The artist living entirely within his art mocks the metamorphosis: "As cultivated flowers turn their stamina to petals so does he turn the practick part to idle show." By setting his optical and practical selves against each other, even making it appear until the final scene that Napoleon might carry the day, Emerson submits his literary vocation to a final and decisive test.

The tendency of *Representative Men* already begins to suggest itself in the chapter on Plato, whose ideas win reverence, but whose shape is never so solid as that of Socrates, an Athenian good old boy, affecting "low phrases" and going off in search of new dialogues after drinking "a whole party under the table." Swedenborg, like Emerson, is "painfully aware of the difference between knowing and doing." He is great in proposing a symbolic language to mediate between heaven and earth, but flawed in making too much of his angels and insisting upon exotic dogma. Montaigne's "vascular speech" comes on as the authoritative idiom of *Representative Men*. While his skepticism deflates the obsessions of either spiritualist or materialist, his best hits are reserved for "the professors," "the skipping ghosts," the angels before their time. In the non-literary Shakespeare, the poet of 1844 has grown several shades more secular. Neither poetic nor dramatic form interests Emerson now, but rather the writer's relation to his culture. Napoleon, the man of action, is quoted more often than Shakespeare, more often than any of the other heroes, and though restricted to the material plane he more nearly resembles Emerson's poet than Shakespeare. Napoleon, too, speaks the language of the masses, and his words become acts; he is the liberator, unfixing things and rearranging matter. "If the poet write a true drama, then he is Caesar and not the player of Caesar." As autobiographical drama, the chapter comes very close to Ovid's transformation of Caesar into a star, until at last Emerson trumps greatness with moral principle and elects another role.

The final juxtaposition of Napoleon and Goethe, both men of their time and adequate to its challenge, decides what sort of fruit will be sufficient. The man of action is overmatched by the writer because he fails to see himself becoming the slave of his action. In his "formidable independence" Goethe takes away "the reproach of weakness" which might otherwise have indicted all works of intellect in the age of Napoleon. The writer's heroism is not monomaniacal, but truly metamorphic. "His failures are the preparation of his victories," says Emerson in an almost purely autobiographical sentence. When crisis instructs him that "all he has yet learned and written is exoteric," he keeps his pen by, then writes in whatever "new light" comes to him. "Artistic but not artist, spiritual but not spiritualist," Goethe makes the strongest possible argument that the writer is indeed a man of action and that his essential act is to make sane words that measure the particular frenzy of his time. Society has "no graver interest" than the preservation at its center of his "comprehensive eye." In his final metamorphosis, Emerson is neither preacher nor poet, but simply writer, accepting the givens of his temperament and the prison of glass which was his vocation.

V

It was understandable that during our own period of enthusiasm the Emerson who said, "But do your own thing and I shall know you," should have seemed especially prominent. But the total circuit of his development argues against identifying him with any one of his sentences or provisional roles. A society whose potential for regeneration has, for the first time, been called seriously into doubt cannot afford to read Emerson selectively. At the same time, and much against his wishes, Emerson has become part of literary history. We cannot always be opening his coffin. An Emersonian sense of the metamorphosis should always prompt a search for the writer who participates in the historical process while commanding it through the imagination and who is never content to be merely literary; whose books are acts, and advances.

Not to speak of metempsychosis, there is, for example, Saul Bellow, whose development and sense of vocation are only slightly more Emersonian than several of his individual works. The force of *The Adventures of Augie March*, a book about "the nobility syndrome," springs from its language, the idiom of a Jewish-urban Montaigne, and from its hero's sustained potential for metamorphosis, his ability to move through a series of transformations while retaining a central self. As the novel's eye, Augie "soaks in the heavy nourishing air" and rests in an Emersonian state "where you are not a subject matter but sit in your own nature, tasting original tastes as good as the first man. . . ." Augie never really expects "the daily facts to go, toil or prisons to go" but his appetite for something special in the way of identity leaves him open to the charge of being "ambitious in general." "You have to be concrete," he is told. "Now Napoleon was. Goethe was."

Great in transition, Bellow is greatest in *Herzog*, a novel that tests and exhibits the American Metamorphosis for its generation as the mature Emerson did for his. The novel's hero is "an unemployed consciousness" whose talk and percipience have been cut off from use and fruitfulness sometime since he delivered the senior class oration on a text from Emerson. Heart and intellect no longer connect in Herzog, a "fool of ideas" in Emerson's phrase, whose definitive study of the Romantic error of the self proves a nearly fatal operation on himself. He has Emerson's gift for the insincerity of multiple moods and for oscillating within a double consciousness, aware from the outside that his closely clutched notion of individuality may be widely viewed as "a persistent infantile megalomania," while trapped inside inescapable selfhood. A cripple, Herzog watches a more agile cripple take his wife; aching for a change of heart "in the serene air of metamorphic New York," he is compelled to be audience to his wife's theatrical conversion to Catholicism. Herzog's American credentials are, as he says, "in good order." He falls and rises again, finds himself convicted, Puritan-fashion, by the Law, and returns to the woods, where his heart is "released from its grisly heaviness and encrustation." Having lived too much in words, he relishes at the last his metamorphosis into silence.

Later Bellow is like later Emerson, a shifting of weight to the other foot. Mr. Sammler, all his becoming behind him, lives on with half-vision, uncertain that in his role as "old-fashioned sitting sage" he will be "strong enough not to be terrified by local effects of metamorphosis, to live with disintegration. . . ." Consciousness, diminished in scope and ambition, keeps a death watch over a friend, the city, possibly the planet. But in doing so it discharges honorably the terms of its unequal contract, which stipulates that a distinguished consciousness shall persist into a society in which all its objects will be vulgar and absurd. No matter, the one good eye ranks, orders, and disposes, even under a shower of excrement. "The spirit knows that its growth is the real aim of existence," says Sammler. "Besides, mankind cannot be something else."

Especially in *Mr. Sammler's Planet*, Bellow recognizes what Emerson rarely brought himself to admit, that men do much to arrange their own tyrannous circumstance, if not as Napoleon then as latter day illuminati, exhorting to "collective ecstasies of news, crisis, power." One may therefore exaggerate too easily the similarities in their themes, but not, I think, in their conception of the responsibilities of the writer. The writer distinguishes between fruitful symbols for the self and what Sammler calls "contrived individuality, bad pastiche." He alerts us to the death rattle when he hears it and to signs of life even if he must invent them. The writer nourishes the metamorphosis.

James M. Cox

R. W. EMERSON: THE CIRCLES OF THE EYE

EMERSON IS DOUBTLESS as visible as he has ever been in the University. Before the advent of American literature as a "subject," he may have enjoyed a wider reputation as venerated presence in the society at large. Before the existence of that venerated presence there had been Emerson, a venerable presence himself, no longer brooding over Concord but dying in it after the Civil War; before that, there had been Emerson the lecturer, spending himself on lyceum circuit forays as an apostle of culture; and before the lecturer there had been the original Emerson, the preacher and writer who had, sixty years after the Declaration of Independence, set out to liberate the imagination of himself and his countrymen. It is surprising how quickly we are led back through these generations of Emerson as object of study through Emerson as genteel cultural presence through Emerson as Concord Sage through Emerson as cultural circuit rider to Emerson the Seer—the veritable eye of God and Self and Nature. How quickly, in other words, we are led back to the transparent eyeball through which Emerson originally declared his vision.

That metaphor—or was it a symbol?—was in its way everything for Emerson. It was as much, let us say, as Whitman's outsetting assertion

> I celebrate myself,
> And what I assume you shall assume
> For every atom belonging to me as good belongs to you

was to be for Whitman. Having imagined so much, Emerson must have felt that everything was possible. Of course everything *wasn't* possible; if so much hadn't flowed from Emerson's outsetting announcement, the whole passage in *Nature* might be little more than a fine instance of a young idealist's whistling in the dark. Yet even if nothing had followed, surely, were we to encounter the passage among the papers of an unknown theological aspirant, we would hear the ring of prophetic assurance in this announcement of a symbolic identity. Indeed, when the passage in its earliest form takes shape in Emerson's journal (March 19, 1835), the eyeball metaphor is significantly absent:

> As I walked in the woods I felt what I often feel, that nothing can befal me in life, no calamity, no disgrace (leaving me my eyes) to which Nature will not offer a sweet consolation. Standing on the bare ground with my head bathed by the blithe air, and uplifted into the infinite space, I become happy in my universal relations. The name of the nearest friend sounds then foreign and accidental. I am the heir of uncontained beauty and power. And if then I walk with a companion, he should speak from his Reason to my Reason; that is, both from God. To be brothers, to be acquaintances, master or servant, is then a trifle too insignificant for remembrance. O, keep this humor, (which in your life-time may not come to you twice,) as the apple of your eye. Set a lamp before it in your memory which shall never be extinguished.

Harold Bloom believes that the fear that "the humor may never return creates the extraordinary image of the transparent eyeball, an image impatient with all possibiltiy of loss, indeed less an image than a promise of perpetual repetition." [1] This is good as far as it goes, but it doesn't go far enough. For the fact is that in the passage in *Nature*, the metaphoric eyeball *displaces* the fear—which is quite different from saying that it is created by the fear. Moreover, the fear in the original passage, far from being what we might call an anxious fear, is really a common-sensical fear, laced as it is to the logic of probability. The ringing proclamation of the self as eyeball is an eloquent conclusion, a poetic hyperbole, which serves as a concrete seal of the experience that has just been described. It is a conversion of the "I" into the Eye, of the Self into the Seer.

Ever since Christopher Cranch caricatured Emerson as a monstrous eyeball on two spindly legs, there has been no shortage of persons ready to bear witness to outlandishness in Emerson's original conception. Even Jonathan Bishop, who has written one of the finest books on Emerson, feels that the metaphor represents a lapse in style from the fine description of the "bare common" which initiates the passage.[2] Yet just as Bloom seems to want the original fear to take a higher intensity than the journal passage warrants, Bishop wants the "realistic" or "concrete" Emerson to prevail over the oracular and transcendental prophet. In its immediate context—the context of *Nature*—and in the context of Emerson's whole career, the metaphor of Emerson as transparent eyeball at once released and defined Emerson's act of imagination. If the metaphor did not cause Emerson to be what he was, it nonethless reveals to us, in the light of what he turned out to be, *who* he was—and the passage

[1] Harold Bloom, "Emerson: The Glory and Sorrows of American Romanticism," in *Romanticism*, ed. David Thorburn and Geoffrey Hartman (Ithaca, 1973), p. 158.

[2] Jonathan Bishop, *Emerson on the Soul* (Cambridge, 1964), pp. 10–15.

in which it first appears is therefore worth concentrated attention:

> Nature is a setting that fits equally well a comic or a mourning piece. In good health, the air is a cordial of incredible virtue. Crossing a bare common, in snow puddles, at twilight, under a clouded sky, without having in my thoughts any occurrence of special good fortune, I have enjoyed a perfect exhilaration. I am glad to the brink of fear. In the woods, too, a man casts off his years, as the snake his slough, and at what period soever of life, is always a child. In the woods is perpetual youth. Within these plantations of God, a decorum and sanctity reign, a perennial festival is dressed, and the guest sees not how he should tire of them in a thousand years. In the woods, we return to reason and faith. There I feel that nothing can befall me in life,—no disgrace, no calamity (leaving me my eyes), which nature cannot repair. Standing on the bare ground,—my head bathed by the blithe air and uplifted into infinite space,—all mean egotism vanishes. I become a transparent eyeball; I am nothing; I see all; the currents of the Universal Being circulate through me; I am part or parcel of God. The name of the nearest friend sounds then foreign and accidental: to be brothers, to be acquaintances, master or servant, is then a trifle and a disturbance. I am the lover of uncontained and immortal beauty. In the wilderness, I find something more dear and connate than in streets or villages. In the tranquil landscape, and especially in the distant line of the horizon, man beholds somewhat as beautiful as his own nature.

In its immediate context, the context of the paragraph in which it appears, the metaphor is the climax of the description of the writer's perception of Nature—that section of Nature which is itself entitled 'Nature"—and is thus the "nature" of *Na-*

ture ⌐ In one sense, the metaphor is the symbolic transformation of the subject, the writer, into an identity equivalent to the state of being, a heightened gladness to the brink of fear, which has been experienced on the twilit bare common. As equivalent, it is a metaphor in the traditional sense. Or we might, following Bloom, call it an image. But in another sense, it is an *action*, a declaration of a change from being to seeing. The metaphor instantaneously transforms being into seeing; if it does not annihilate personal consciousness, it causes the personal experience to vanish by virtue of the expansion and uplift of the essential self into infinite space: "I am nothing. I see all." Moreover, there is a paradoxical relation between the eyeball and the infinite space it occupies. Since the eyeball is transparent and cannot be seen—is in effect an invisible organizing film presumably containing the universe, through which and in which the currents of the Universal Being circulate—it should be coextensive with the infinite universe. Yet the eyeball metaphor is nonetheless concrete, an assertion of infinite existence in a definite image. That paradox was not something Emerson sought to realize as an aspect of style—he particularly disliked that characteristic of Thoreau's writing. Rather, it was an expression of the essential relation between language and Nature. It was the inevitable and miraculous necessity of a true—that is, a poetic—language to assert the radical relationship between thought and thing. That is why Emerson did not, at his best, use metaphor decoratively and why, in this crucial instance, he did not say he became *like* a transparent eyeball. The transforming power of metaphor is, for Emerson, the active spiritualizing power of language—it is the God acting as language—and Emerson's becoming a transparent eyeball is his master metaphor. This transformation is a fatally idealizing process in which mean egotism becomes nothing, whereupon nothing can befall me in life. . . . The name of the nearest friend sounds then foreign and accidental: to be brothers, to be acquaintances, master or servant, is then a trifle and a disturbance.

Yet for all the idealizing in Emerson's act of vision, the metaphor keeps the vision from being totally subjective. It is subjective in the sense that the consciousness in the form of the eyeball in effect contains everything. Still, there *is* the metaphor, which carries Emerson outside himself. The mean ego has vanished in order for Nature to exist. To be sure, it is impossible to tell whether Eye or Nature comes first. In the sequence of the entire passage, Nature precedes the eye, though it is clear that, by becoming part or parcel of God, the Eye sees Nature—as if God passed through the Eye to create Nature. All three entities—God, Man, and Nature—clearly interpenetrate each other, and Emerson's logic throughout the essay wants to place them in an equal relationship. That is why both the argument and direction of the entire essay bend to embrace that equality; it is also why the initial eyeball metaphor is the instantaneous enactment of the whole idea of Nature. The metaphor is, after all, the image of the imagination seeing nature, and the essay is not only the elaboration but the result of that vision.

While Emerson's logic is equalizing, or attempting to equalize, God and Man and Nature, at the same time his rhetorical bias, his inheritance of traditional religious language, and his transformation via transcendence all combine to form a current of relentless idealization of Nature. Thus Emerson's movement in the essay is from the "low" commodity of Nature up through aesthetic to moral and intellectual beauty, through language, through discipline and on to idealism. These terms constitute the very ladder of his aspirational vision. Yet however much

Emerson's impulse is to idealize Nature, he has to reject idealism because it would degrade Nature into phenomena and thereby deny the existence of the very entity he has set out to redeem; it would, as he says late in the essay, "leave me in the splendid labyrinth of my perceptions to wander without end."

For that reason, Emerson moves from idealism to the realm of spirit, the active principle of idealism—what we might call thought in motion—which sends up and illuminates the Universe. Spirit is, of course, God—the Supreme Being which, according to Emerson, "puts forth Nature through Us." But Nature is, by virtue of the passage through us, like the human body, an inferior incarnation of God, a projection of God in the unconscious. Spirit is the impulse which organizes and gives direction and purpose to Nature; its equivalent in style is the imperative, hortatory, moral tone which characterizes Emerson's prose, inspiring him to radical metaphor but also constantly threatening to weaken the power in Nature which he seeks.

For Nature, that which the transparent eyeball at once sees and contains, must be, like the eye which sees it, radically there. And like the eye which sees it, the limits of nature are infinite; indeed, despite the solitary pastoral setting in which Emerson sees it, Nature really can include society. Though the solitude has the benignant aspects bestowed upon it by the equally benignant and idealized Nature, there is outside the perimeter of the eye the negative world of the vanished ego—the world which Emerson can, as the mood moves him, cast outside or inside nature. It is the world of talent rather than genius, convention rather than originality, the past rather than the present, the church rather than God, institutions rather than men—in a word, it is society rather than the essential self in Nature. It forms the negative but highly necessary background which affords Emerson an instantaneous perceptual dialectic, enabling him to pour positive energy into his charmed field of vision and thus dramatize the original power so necessary to keep the idealizing impulse invigorated.

So what we have in *Nature* is a declaration of independence not so much from society as in society—for it is society which surrounds Emerson. After all, it is a *bare common* from which Emerson soars into his new identity. Moreover, the bare common was not present in the journal entry. To be sure, Emerson allows himself free passage from bare common to Nature's woods in his movement toward his ultimate assertion. Even so, he clearly has that bare common much in mind when he says, at the very threshold of translating himself into a visionary, "Standing on the bare ground . . . all mean egotism vanishes." [3]

Thus, in his first essay, however much Emerson sought to define Nature, he meant to possess the ground from which he could see society. This twilight walker is occupying the space at the center of the village, not to reject the village, not to reform it, as much as to envision it in the fullest sense of the word. For all the infinite space which Emerson occupies wth his metaphor, he is still on that bare common, and his whole aim, located as he is at the center of society, is to free himself to become the center—to possess the *common* nature possessed by the village and make it something more than bare. The possession is not of course in terms of legal, material ownership—the village and town already own it materially—but in terms of a vision which

[3] Emerson had, at the very outset of *Nature*, shown his disposition to move freely between the *common* and the *philosophical* sense of nature, a point I shall emphasize later in the discussion. His movement here from the bare common to the sanctified transcendental woods, though it can be seen as the vagueness of rapture, seems to me to exemplify a determined freedom from being fixed in nature as place.

will discover the force of Nature which exists not only on the bare common but also in the heart of the sleeping society. By being the veritable pupil of Nature, Emerson will be the true teacher of society. The bare common is therefore the crucial ground on which Emerson stands; to realize it is to recover the full meaning of Emerson's decision, at the outset of *Nature*, "to use the word [nature] in both senses;—in its common and in its philosophical import. The *common* sense of Nature is, as Emerson says, those essences unchanged by man, whereas all those constructions of man—houses, roads, canals, towns—fall under the heading of Art. By deliberately refusing to deny this common sense of Nature, even though it would *exclude* the bare common from the realm of the natural and place it in the realm of the artistic and social, Emerson means to subject the common sense of Nature as well as the bare common to full re-vision.

The whole argument of Emerson's first essay is thus rooted in the instantaneous act of the metaphor which precedes the argument. Jonathan Bishop in discussing Emerson's style wisely observes that Emerson knew that a man's metaphors mean what they say.[4] Surely this one, as much as any Emerson ever imagined, bears witness to that observation. The initial metaphor foretells the conclusion of *Nature* in which Emerson says

> The problem of restoring to the world original and eternal beauty is solved by the redemption of the soul. The ruin or blank that we see in nature is in our own eye. The axis of vision is not coincident with the axis of things, and so they appear not transparent but opaque.

And he goes on to say that once we have integrated spirit and matter into their original unity then we will look at the world

[4] Bishop, *Emerson on the Soul*, pp. 119–128. Bishop's entire discussion of Emerson's concern with, use of, and committment to metahor is excellent.

with new eyes. He even evokes his Orphic Poet to proclaim in the last sentences of *Nature:*

> As when the summer comes from the south the snow banks melt and the face of the earth becomes green before it, so shall the advancing spirit create its ornaments along its path, and carry with it the beauty it visits and the song which enchants it; it shall draw beautiful faces, warm hearts, wise discourse, and heroic acts, around its way, until Evil is no more seen. The kingdom of man over nature, which cometh not with observation—a dominion such as now is beyond his dream of God,—he shall enter without more wonder than the blind man feels who is gradually restored to perfect sight.

Though the poetic utterance gives us once again the metaphor of vision, it is nonetheless flaccid. The "as when . . . so shall" construction is far from the swift, spirited oracular language of the essay. Of course Emerson could say—really does say—that it is not himself but his Orphic Poet speaking, but that is an insufficient defense. If the Poet is Bronson Alcott, then why choose Alcott, if he can do no better than this? Besides, it isn't Alcott; it is Emerson, run beyond his true ending into weak vision and weak language. Here is indeed vapidity, and it occurs the moment Emerson enters a "heavenly" realm in which there is not the sharp resistance of those opaque things. In such a realm, Emerson is in the resistless air of spirit, and the world of Nature is always at the threshold of becoming a weakly poeticized prospect rather than a strongly imagined figure of spirit.

If we take Emerson, standing on the bare common, become an eye at the natural center of society to see and thereby recreate it, we have the essential Emerson—the Emerson of *Nature* imagined by himself at the outset of his career as the fixed center of the existent universe. He had his essential thought, as Kenneth Cameron has shown; [5] he had a style to match his vision, a style in which metaphor (itself the visible presence, in language, of thought in the act of becoming image) at once preceded and made possible his argument; and he had his role, that of teacher and preacher to the townsmen he would instruct and exhort; finally he had his form, the essay, which through his eye was an experiment in vision—an urgent perception intent upon disclosing the unity of man and nature. Since Emerson was a writer, not an artist, his seeing perforce had to be saying. What Emerson sought in style was a rhythm and a decisiveness which would equal the perception he was proclaiming. Discursive argument was largely closed to him, for his initial position put him out of linear logic, a point Sherman Paul decisively made twenty years ago; [6] his poetic, symbolic, or metaphoric identity—call it what we will—kept his language constantly charged with affect; his denial of time, in favor of circular repetition, drove him toward compression and epigrammatic execution of thought and away from expansion, discursiveness, exposition, or narrative, which he felt were enslaved to clarity, the mere light of the understanding.

His vision sought to pierce through the surface of Nature and Man and literally review the traditional terms, the essential generalizations which form the permanent structure of man in society. The very titles of his successive series of essays display his central concerns: History, Self-Reliance, Compensation, Spiritual Laws, Love, Friendship, Prudence, Heroism, the

[5] Kenneth Cameron, *Emerson the Essayist*, 2 vols. (Raleigh, 1945). The first volume amply documents the influences upon and development of Emerson's thought up to and including the publication of *Nature*.

[6] Sherman Paul, *Emerson's Angle of Vision* (Cambridge, 1952), pp. 5–26.

Over-Soul, Circles, Intellect, The Poet, Experience, Character, Manners, Gifts, Nature (not the original essay but a subsequent and quite subordinate attempt on the term), Politics, and Nominalist and Realist.

These are what I choose to call the Circles of the Eye. It is no more an accident that the one geometric form to which Emerson devotes an essay is the circle than that that essay should begin with the following sentences:

> The eye is the first cirle; the horizon which it forms is the second; and throughout nature this primary figure is repeated without end. It is the highest emblem in the cipher of the world.

There is the Emersonian style at its finest—a strong, unqualified assertion, followed by another and yet another. The second two assertions are in once sense restatements of the first one, though they are just as clearly consequences of it. And the third is at once declarative and metaphoric. That word *cipher* does a world of work. For the cipher is of course a zero, an empty arithmetic circle which, placed at the right of, or following a number, increases its value tenfold. And it is also a coding, a symbolic reading, which discovers meaning. The sentences, sufficiently independent to be epigrammatic, create a momentary but decisive gap between each other, which the eye and ear of the reader and listener bridge with a responsive intellectual leap of energy. Moreover, the metaphoric third sentence is not illustrative, but equivalent, as if it were inevitably called forth. In a fine way, the metaphor is buried, or rooted in the very sense of the passage. It is, in other words, a third and final circle of the primary eye. How quickly all this is done, and how completely. Begin an essay this way, and how can you fail?

Well, you can fail even so, and Emerson sometimes does

fail, though certainly not in this essay. It is one of his best—short, fierce, and utterly complete. The "I" of the author is fully converted into the reading eye of the reader. Emerson does not see for us but sees through, by means of us. The connections we have to make to discover the full sequence are by no means free association; they are the fated spatial silences between the sentences, instinct with implicit energy—dots, we might say, which when connected form the circle of the essay. Emerson ends on the following note:

> The one thing which we seek with insatiable desire is to forget ourselves, to be surprised out of our propriety, to lose our sempiternal memory and to do something without knowing how or why; in short to draw a new circle. Nothing great was ever achieved without enthusiasm. The way of life is wonderful; it is by abandonment. The great moments of history are the facilities of performance through the strength of ideas, as the works of genius and religion. "A man," said Oliver Cromwell, "never rises so high as when he knows not whither he is going." Dreams and drunkenness, the use of opium and alcohol are the semblance and counterfeit of this oracular genius, and hence their dangerous attraction for men. For the like reason they ask the aid of wild passions, as in gaming and war, to ape in some manner these flames and generosities of the heart.

I have not quoted the passage for the presence of a final circle in it, though it is good to see Emerson strongly return to his primary figure. Nor is it quoted for possessing the utterly typical absolute assertion: "Nothing great was ever achieved without enthusiasm." That is an example of the Emersonian sentiment of assurance executed as epigram; yet for all its absoluteness, it is nonetheless the expression of a mood, and Emerson has already said in this very essay that "our moods do not believe in each other." Emerson knows quite well outside the circle of this essay that something great might be achieved without enthusiasm. But that would be another circle—possibly the circle of Prudence, or Wealth, or Manners, or Politics.

No, not for these is the passage exquisite, but for the rare, and in its movement, the daring ending—the abrupt illumination of Cromwell's somewhat grandiose utterance in terms of drunkenness, opium, and alcohol. Here is a swift and pungent explanation of rankly sensual behavior under the aegis of the idealized statement. The abruptness, which is to say the instantaneous decision, of the move sends life and meaning in both directions. For Cromwell's statement depicts a stage of drunkenness—a not knowing where one is going—just as the state of actual drunkenness is also some effort to get out of oneself. Such a fine blunt move seems to me a genuine realization of Emerson's contention at the outset of the passage that "we seek with an insatiable desire . . . to be surprised out of our propriety." The sudden juxtaposition of the two activities; the sequence, which is to say the direction, from high to low; and the relationship, so much of which is left implicit or silent in the momentary space between the sentences—all combine to charge the field.

These sentences of Emerson are like atoms; they are striving to be worlds of their own; they bear out again and again in the action of their form his endless plea for the present to prevail over the past, and are thus repeatedly executing his central theme, just as their self-containment repeats his central figure. The high mind—even the high-mindedness—of Emerson is always present, even dominant; it is the resonance of his tone. But its swift reach into the so-called material aad instinctual world is richly audacious. These descents of the spirit are as fraught with ecstasy as any ascent Emerson could make. They not only promise but recover a wildness of spirit. Such conversions of spirit to Nature are the perceptions of the transparent eye.

The Emersonian sentence, charged with its atomic independent impulse—he once referred to his sentences as infinitely repellent particles—is the analogue for the essay which struggles to contain it. For the essays are the larger self-contained circles which stand by themselves, yet are bound to each other by the larger silent spaces between them. In a way they are all repetitions of *Nature*, for Emerson is an alarmingly repetitive writer. And these silent spaces between the essays are the vanished mean ego—the first-person pronoun of Emerson—which has become the charged space wherein we connect or leap the gap from essay to essay. We might even say that the vanished mean ego, the *biography* of Emerson, which has literally dissolved into the spaces between the intense intuitional moments of vision which literally are the essays, is admonished into silence by the voice of vision, the sayings of the seer. After all, Emerson's essays are self-directions as much as they are directions to an audience. No, not quite as much, for the hortatory tone of the preacher attempting to lift us out of ourselves represents a balance of admonition flowing outward in the form of address.

This vision of the essays as circles of the central eye is of course nothing but a metaphor—yet I mean for it to have consequences.

First of all, the repeated conversion of the "I" into the Eye cannot be taken lightly. There is enormous psychological cost in such an idealizing process. If the "I" and all the personalities which existed around Emerson in time and place—his parents, his brothers, his wives, his children—are not annihilated, they are threatened with consumption by the vision. There is a sense in which Emerson literally feeds off the death of those around him. Before he wrote *Nature* he had already lost two brothers and a first wife, all victims of tuberculosis, and he himself hovered at the threshold of consumption during his early life. Breath, which is our literal physical experience of the spirit of life, was thus crucial, even desperate, to Emerson; hence the astonishing literal force in his use of the verbs *inspire, transpire, conspire, expire, aspire.* There is, for example, a felt relation between his bursts of inspiration and the death of his first wife. If he does not exult in her death, there is nonetheless an influx of energy consequent on her passing—an imaginative energy boldly evident in the journal. Her spiritualization, which Emerson's traditional religious attitude embraces, makes her a part of the air he breathes. And the clear despair which he records on the loss of his brother Charles is but a prelude to the strong assertion of *Nature.* Getting out of the "I," the personal pronoun, and getting over the deaths of loved ones is no tired or traditional "spiritual" vision for Emerson precisely because it is a literal breathing in, or inspiration, of the death of life.

Moreover, there is in Emerson's bold assertions of self-confidence a threat to everyone around him. In the face of prior disasters and griefs, even if we grant that his second marriage and the birth of a son may have given him needed assurance for launching himself as a writer, Emerson's assertion of an idealized metaphoric self which, short of blindness, would be impervious to any evil, has about it a ferocious element of provocation. If Margaret Fuller had proclaimed her acceptance of the Universe, Emerson had both stared and dared it to its face. Implicit in his contention that no evil can befall him in his form of transparent eyeball is a challenge to the Universe to do what it will, since he can see by himself. How glad we should be that he at least had the grace and wit and common sense to exempt his eyes, both of them, from his all but absolute act of pride!

Looking at the statement from another point of view, we could say that if we had been little Waldo and had been precocious enough, we would have wished to say before we were five years old, "Father, *why* did you say such a thing?" For if Emerson was austerely coming out of evil, he was at the same time asking for more. It would be the fuel for his flame. How have pride and not be stricken? And no amount of transforming pride into obedience can quite charm Emerson's circle unless rude Nature and violent spirit are surging within it. Otherwise, it will be just a charming circle in the form of a decorative metaphor.

There is thus, I think, in Emerson's fine sentences early in *Nature*, an implicit sentence of death for little Waldo. And indeed, can we, looking at Emerson's life, wish that Waldo had lived? Can we really imagine he would have grown up to be a flaming independent imagination? Emerson's other children hardly fared well. There was Ellen Tucker Emerson, named for the dead first wife as if she were to be an admonition to Lydia (who had herself suffered a renaming as Lydian to get her out of the unfortunate New England vernacular pronunciation), who took care of the Concord Sage in his declining years. There was Edith Emerson, whose husband, W. H. Forbes, helped Emerson with his finances and securities. And finally there was Edward Waldo Emerson, inheritor of the sickly Emersonian constitution who couldn't go to the Civil War—was indeed actively denied his wish to go by his concerned parents—and who was left to edit Mr. Emerson's journals. He did creditable work, I think we could say, but every line of his prose affirms his role as undertaker of the body of Emerson's work. Whatever vengeance was in the children lay in building a sepulchre of the father. The true children of Emerson were elsewhere. Born of the seeds of language, Thoreau and Whitman, Emily Dickinson and Robert Frost (and Frank Lloyd Wright and Charles Ives too), were wild, recalcitrant embodiments of the Emersonian spirit, flaming by the ponds and in the cities, villages, and fields of the republic.

I am not higgling about Emerson's failure to be a good parent—whoso would higgle, let him dare to have children and know what it is to possess them. I simply wish to welcome the fate which was in Emerson's freedom, the death in his life. Already in *Nature* he had said at the end of the section on discipline (which precedes the section on idealism):

> When much intercourse with a friend has supplied us with a standard of excellence, and has increased our respect for the resources of God who thus sends a real person to outgo our ideal; when he has, moreover, become an object of thought, and whilst his character retains all its unconscious effect, is converted in the mind into solid and sweet wisdom,—it is a sign to us that his office is closing, and he is commonly withdrawn from our sight in a short time.

Biographically considered, that passage clearly refers to Charles, who had just died. But it just as clearly looks forward to the passage in "Experience," which deals with the death of Waldo. Logically considered, the passage unremittingly defines the terms of the transparent eyeball. Seeing a friend is at once a conversion of life into thought, a *taking* of life. And if such seeing is to continue, more life is going to have to be taken. To be sure, in the sweet dialectic of transcendence, thought has preceded life anyway and can be declared as the more intense conception and conclusion of life. Yet Emerson's prose is never as sweet as it may look. He himself wanted bite and sting and decision in prose.

This vision of Emerson's Eye in relation to his personal life may seem appalling, yet I think much of the writing on Emerson discloses attitudes which could well be considered expressions of precisely this vision held *unconsciously*. There is, for example, a distinct wish expressed by critics of Emerson that his personal life should have been more of a trial of his ideas than it actually was. Thus there is even a downright resentment about his "success," his too serene middle years. Similarly, there is, on the part of those who praise Emerson, a slight lament that he lost something of his early fire when his house became warm and comfortable.

All of which brings me to the second consequence of seeing Emerson's essays as the circles of his Eye. For all the change which Emerson celebrated—remember that the currents of the Universal Being are constantly circulating through the transparent eyeball—the Eye is just as constantly fixed. Though Emerson can look on the faces of Nature, the tyrannous Unity must assert itself and be asserted again and again. I do not see Emerson as "developing" or "progressing" or "declining." Of course he declined into old age; of course he finally lost his energy (he had always maintained that he had never been given enough to begin with); but he lived long enough as a writer to make it necessary for those who posit a decline to bury him prematurely in order to confirm their vision.

Nor do those who see Emerson as somehow discovering more reality than he first bargained for fare much better. If the one party tends to see Emerson as a revolutionary who slumped into society, the second tends to see him as an emerging Realist whose initial dream was superseded by experience. Stephen Whicher, who regretted a bit too much the absence of evil in Emerson, wishes to rescue the later Emerson, the Emerson who faced the fate of his earlier freedom. Jonathan Bishop, on the other hand, finds the early Emerson sounding the bolder note and receding through the crises of Waldo's death into the prac-

tical world of *The Conduct of Life*. And now Quentin Anderson
appears to applaud Bishop's evaluation of the early Emerson as
the more revolutionary, but to assert that the revolution was a
mistake. Anderson has seen the student riots, the Vietnam War,
the imperial American expansion into Asia, and, implicitly as
well as explicitly relating this recent history to the Emersonian
imagination, he deplores the imperial Emersonian self, which he
sees as what he calls a "coming out of culture." [7]

There is no doubt that the early Emerson is central; Emerson was in effect all there at the beginning and all that he was to
do was implicit in the metaphoric identity he proclaimed for
himself. Of course he had experience; of course he saw things in
life which he could not quite have foreseen at the outset. But
visions of Emerson's career in terms of crises and turning points,
in ups and downs, in directions from revolution to compromise
or from idealism to realism have their own distortion. That
there was entropy of energy I am delighted to acknowledge, but
never the kind of entropy which could not produce the old flame
from the slow decay.

Indeed, locating Emerson's revolutionary power in his early
years causes Anderson to distort the image of the outsetting
Emerson. Emerson never was so revolutionary as Anderson
wishes to have him. He had from the very beginning a deeply
conservative quality. He was right on that bare common in the
center of village culture. It was the eccentric Thoreau who occupied the ground at the edge of the village. If Emerson had
revolted against the church, it was nonetheless a one-man revolt
which Emerson never wanted vulgarized into a movement.
Thus he was not asking the divinity students to leave the church
but to be themselves within it and thereby renew it. Emerson is

[7] Quentin Anderson, *The Imperial Self* (New York, 1971), pp.
201–244.

always aware that society exists; he very much wants it to exist; he has no real doubt that it will continue to exist; he is very much aware that the very isolate position he assumes in relation to it is just that—in *relation* to it, and therefore in a deep way, deep enough to be rooted in instinctual consciousness, dependent upon society as an entity all but equal to whatever self he can ever assert.

It is true that he is always determined to affirm the self over society, but the affirmation always has the ring of exhortation. The appeal in Emerson's imperatives is a recognition that the balance of power is on society's side and must always be proclaimed for the self precisely because it has been so fatally surrendered. There is from the beginning a margin of safety on the bare common which has somehow been secured by law and is therefore a sanctuary, a new church to move into. Thus Emerson is calling to us to rely on ourselves out of a profound recognition that we will not and have not; the ringing of his bell is a reminder of what we could but will probably never be. What keeps Emerson strongly present beneath the ringing of that bell is his solid grasp of the fate—the persistent and repeated form—of society. By getting out of history, Emerson wants to see the external stability of change almost as much as he wants to accomplish the change of getting out. The self he proclaims has about it no small measure of tradition; it is a recovery as well as a departure.

Emerson's very language embraces the traditional aspect of speech. He does not want a new language so much as he wants a renewal of the existing language. He loves proverbs and is delighted to see new experience conform to the traditional, proverbial, common wisdom. If he earnestly desires to lodge his own proverbs in the language, he nonetheless knows that he has chosen the proverb and the epigram as the desired form into which to cast himself. That is an inextricable aspect of his aphoristic and oracular style. For all his ringing insistence that man is innocent instead of originally sinful, Emerson wants the innocent self to be a conscience—a new conscience to be sure, but withal a conscience. Hence the admonitory aspect of his essays. Emerson's blessed encouragement is, as everyone knows who reads him, both accompanied by and charged with admonition. His uplift is not without squelch. Consciousness is forever at the threshold of becoming conscience. The teacher is always about to be the preacher; the lecture or the essay is never far from being the sermon. The Emersonian sentence is sufficiently instinct with judgment to carry conviction.

Emerson's whole drive toward unity, toward circularity, illustrates this conservative element in his imagination. For the circle, however much it may be impelled to expand, is seeking both to include and to contain all of experience rather than to reject and destroy it. The two eyes which become one in transparent sight integrate rather than divide the field of vision. The very fact that vision is Emerson's metaphor of thought makes him know the aspect of illusion which dwells in the realm of what he would call reality. If it is inevitable that he should have written an essay on circles it is equally inevitable that he should have written one on illusions. What is great about Emerson is his willingness to expose and thereby anticipate the illusoriness of his own thought. The bullet-like force of his self-relying sentences always threatens to put the reality of the preceding sentence in jeopardy.

There is a deep impulse in Emerson to declare everything as an illusion—everything. The question which then stands up to this hard Yankee pressure is "What is the most powerful illusion?" The answer is, I think, the central self, that transparent eye of consciousness. Yet because even it is ultimate vision it

has an element of illusion in it—which is far different from saying that it is necessarily unreal or illusory. Surely Emerson's
repeated and memorable admonition to *trust* the self betrays in
its very terminology the appeal at the heart of the imperative.
The appeal is for every man to believe in and assent to those
momentary flashes in experience when issues appear clear, when
emotion is translated into adequate action, when thought seems
the very double of the body. The motion of the body is, when it
moves instinctively beneath the sway of mind, the double of the
will and is our primary experience of Nature instinct with
thought.

This illusion of a central self is so persistent that Emerson is
willing to risk all on its being a reality. And so the central self is
the anchor of essays so apparently disparate as "Self-Reliance,"
"Experience," and "Fate." "Self-Reliance" is a buoyant call to
trust those intuitional moments when perception—which for
Emerson is instantaneous thought—yields total presence, blot-
ting out the image of the self in relation to society (which is conformity) and the image of the self in relation to past experience
(which is consistency). "Experience," on the other hand, instead
of exhorting to self-trust, rushes headlong through the categories
of perception, which Emerson denominates Illusion, Temperament, Succession, Surface, Surprise, Reality, and Subjectiveness. These are the lords of life, the very illusions by means
of which man creates his existence. Indeed *experience* is, as Emerson sees it in what seems to me the most exhilarating of all his
essays, the swift exposure of these dominant categories of perception—what we rely on as our ideas of life—as illusions.
These forms of perception are the means by which we tempo-
rarily fix Nature only to see it burst into another life. Without
the fix, the *idea* of Nature or Life, we cannot see it, yet the
moment form gives our vision identity, Nature dances into life

again. There is nothing left at the last—after the successive
disillusions—but the sanity of the self which creates the illusory
lords of life. Thus, if "Self-Reliance" was a ringing exhortation
to trust the self, "Experience" turns out to disclose that, after
the last disillusion of experience, there is nothing else to rely on
but the self, of which Emerson bravely says: "We must hold
hard to this poverty, however scandalous, and by more repeated
self-recoveries, after the sallies of action, possess our axis more
firmly." That axis is surely the volatile line relating Experience
to Self-Reliance, and the two essays are really its poles. If the
one is positive and the other negative, they are the alternations
of a single current of energy. And surely "Fate," far from being
a change in Emerson's central philosophy, is a change in perspective. Once Fate is seen—and Emerson burns with all his
original energy as he sees it—then Self-Reliance is once more
possible. For the man who can humbly accept his destiny can
even recklessly obey his impulses.

To believe in the self enables a person to see society more
than it makes him wish to reject or even reform it. Every person
must see it by and for himself; otherwise he merely joins a
movement and is engulfed by a party of society. And the seeing
is likely to as brief as it is sure—as brief as a sentence or an
essay. The solitary intensity of vision predicates a stubborn,
conservative, persistent society which will perennially occupy
the interstices between the moments of intuition.

Is Emerson then a conservative? Not on my life. After all
the admonition, the exhortation, the relentless and even fearful
idealization, there is a buoyant hope in Emerson—and buoyant
not because it is hope but because it is shown by Emerson to be
a state of mind which practically exists in every waking day—as
near as the air we breathe. Of course Emerson can be weak and
distant—not merely in his late years but in his early ones too.
He is, as John Jay Chapman astutely remarked, weak on the fine

arts. His overwhelming belief in language prevented him from being able to see visually. Seeing is really always saying in Emerson; perception is always thought. And if Emerson is not weak on love, he is certainly hard on it. Because he sees every self as a circle, two selves can touch at only one point. The more intense the point of contact, the more appetency and hunger which must be aroused at other points along the vast perimeters of the two selves. Thus after all is given to love and particularly when all is given, the self can and must come into its own. Such a view goes hard with romance, with narrative, with the novel. And though Emerson could write on the Comic (how pleasantly surprising that he made the attempt) he hasn't much of a sense of humor. He has no patience with anyone who giggles, and says so in a way to chill the playful heart. He can, after a long session of reading him, seem to have enough moral seriousness about him to make a reader, or this one at least, embrace Mark Twain's contention that the Moral Sense makes us the lowest rather than the highest creatures in God's Kingdom of Nature.

Yet count over his weaknesses as we will—count them over with savage delight—Emerson still sees us, really makes us possible. He was, after all, a prophet, not in predicting the future but in making it happen. He called for a scholar and there was Thoreau. He called for a poet and there was Whitman. Reading Emerson at his best is always a reminder as well as a recognition that I am. I do not know his work well enough. I have not read it all. I have not devoted myself long enough or hard enough to the task of understanding him. But there he is to tell me that there are better things to do than to read him, that I have read enough of him, that I am as good as he is, that I too, at this instant, shall prevail. And all in a voice at once exacting and exhilarating, a voice which, when heard, is proof as well as prompting of my inmost character. Here is no coming out of culture, but a making culture possible.

Phyllis Cole

EMERSON, ENGLAND, AND FATE

THE YEARS AFTER Emerson's second trip to England presented him more than ever with the need for social engagement as a writer and lecturer. With the English crisis of 1848 fresh in mind, he turned his attention back to America during a decade of westward expansion and accelerating conflict over slavery. Now, Emerson thought, was indeed the moment when the scholar must address "the Times." Conducting simultaneous and often comparative studies of England and America, Emerson worked throughout the 1850s toward an understanding of modern society. The results are evident in his two published books of that decade, *English Traits* (1856) and *The Conduct of Life* (1860); but the theme finds important expression in his lectures and journal writings as well.

Emerson saw himself as an unlikely participant in the social forum. A decade earlier he had suggested that the Transcendentalist would proclaim truth to his society more often by silence than by speech, would perform actions only if they were "necessary" and "adequate." [1] By the 1850s, however, closer in-

Note: quotations from Emerson's lecture manuscripts are made with the permission of William H. Bond of Houghton Library and the Ralph Waldo Emerson Memorial Association.

[1] *The Complete Works of Ralph Waldo Emerson*, Centenary Edition,

volvement seemed a necessity. An 1851 journal passage suggests the dilemma:

> The ancients most truly and poetically represented the incarnation or descent into Nature of Pythagoras, his condescension to be born, as his first virtue.
>
> It is indeed a perilous adventure, this serious act of venturing into mortality, swimming in a sea strewn with wrecks, where none indeed go undamaged. It is as bad as going to Congress; none comes back innocent.

Clearly, Emerson-as-Pythagoras still does not see the descent to Nature and Congress as an easy accomplishment. As a present reality it is a struggle amidst wreckage, perhaps even a drowning. But "incarnation" has become a primary virtue as well. "Those who conquer," Emerson concludes, ". . . announce this success in every syllable." [2] A new strength of voice and vision will be the result.

This double theme—the individual's need for incarnation into the world and the danger of being engulfed or entrapped by it—significantly informed all of Emerson's social thinking during these years. He characterized aspects of English and American society in metaphors of material obstruction and enclosure; and he expanded a similar sense of oppression into a cosmic principle, manifested both in nature and in society, when he described "Fate" at the beginning of *The Conduct of Life*. As the Pythagoras passage indicates, Emerson himself felt the oppression he described. But in addition this idea offered to him an important

---

ed. Edward Waldo Emerson (Boston and New York, 1903–1904), I, 350.

[2] *The Journals of Ralph Waldo Emerson*, ed. Edward Waldo Emerson and Waldo Emerson Forbes (Boston and New York, 1909–1919), VIII, 239–240.

measure of larger social vitality: a nation or circumstance could be judged according to its deadening or enlivening effect upon that incarnated individual. I would like to follow these various characterizations of the social world as they mutually inform each other in Emerson's thought throughout the fifties.

England provided Emerson with both a significant experience in the development of a social theory and a crucial theme within it, and it is with his English experience of 1847–48 that I will begin. Like so many of his American contemporaries—Hawthorne and Melville, most notably—Emerson approached travel in England as an exercise in self-definition, responding positively to the source of his own native culture but looking with some nationalistic contentment upon signs of the parent nation's decline. In fact before his 1847 tour Emerson had already worked out in a lecture series the theory about the relationship of England and America that would later form the backbone of *English Traits;* in 1843 he had characterized New England as the heir to England's vital Anglo-Saxon materialism, possessing at the same time a spiritual vitality now waning in England.[3] America, he felt, was both a new England and an anti-England. His trip to England in 1847 was not, then, just another lecture tour and certainly not, as some have said, an admission that his creative work in America was over. It provided for a study of society from the perspective of the potentiality and limitations of modern materialism, and America was only one thought away at all times. Emerson wanted to lecture to British audiences; but, as he wrote home to his wife, his real business there was not speaking in itself but "the faithful seeing

[3] "New England" lecture series; Houghton Library mss., Lectures and Sermons of Ralph Waldo Emerson, 199 (1–5).

of England." [4] For a man committed to the act of "seeing" in its fullest sense, this was important business.

The aspect of Emerson's English experience most important here is the society that appeared later as one of his strong images of the world's limitation on the active visionary capacity of the individual: a machine, a phalanstery, a universal Birmingham of the mind. The base in concrete experience is quite clear: Emerson spent the winter of 1847–48 lecturing in the world's capitals of mechanical power, first in Liverpool and Manchester, then in other cities of the industrial north. As a guest of the Free Trade Liberals, he was in a fine position to meet this society's most eminent men, its political leaders, manufacturers, and intellectuals. And it was their mental and moral qualities that most fascinated him in his journal observations. Emerson did express interest in the financial crisis of that winter and in the social arrangements proposed by these men; he did in fact register moral indignation at English industrial poverty the same decade that men as different as Carlyle, Melville, and Engels did;[5] but his particular question was the quality of mind elicited by such circumstances, the nature of the vision by which the leaders of government and culture would solve problems. Richard Cobden, the leader of the Anti-Corn Law movement, especially fascinated him, for instance, as "the *cor cordis*, the object of honor and belief, to risen and rising England." But soon Emerson realized that for Cobden Free Trade led nowhere, was only a limited practical device and not a principle. Using a simile that

[4] *The Letters of Ralph Waldo Emerson*, ed. Ralph L. Rusk (New York, 1939), III, 461.

[5] See, for instance, *Letters*, III, 442; *Journals and Miscellaneous Notebooks of Ralph Waldo Emerson*, ed. William H. Gilman, et al. (Cambridge, 1960–   ), X, 245; Houghton Library ms. lectures "England" and "London," 201 (1–2).

would take on some importance later in *English Traits*, he wrote in his journal, "Cobden was the better leader for what he did not see; like a horse with blinders." What Emerson was looking for was a British engineer, a master of machines and arrangements, who was not mastered by them—a man of vision as well as utility. George Stephenson, who built one of the first locomotives in England, seemed to possess that vision; and his ability to harness power became a chief metaphor for understanding the needs of the time. Emerson saw society itself as the ultimate object of such genius; and he wrote, "Stephenson executed the idea of the age in iron. Who will do it in the social problem? We want a moral engineer." [6]

That phrase "moral engineer" is crucial, because it is one of Emerson's first suggestions that English society itself is a kind of machine, a locomotive or a mill that might be reconstructed. We certainly see Emerson at his most utilitarian here. But, as one might expect, reservations arise quickly about the possibility or desirability of a new class of "social engineers." In Birmingham that winter Emerson wrote that the cities of industrial England were growing together to form a new kind of urban society bigger than London, and that such "mechanical might" was "oppressive to behold." Going on to London for the spring of 1848, he arrived in time to witness the Chartist uprising of April, and he saw that the "machine" of urban England was seriously malfunctioning both in its basic operations and in its proposed readjustments:

> Pauperism always accrues in English arrangements. Like sediment from brackish water incrusting the locomotive and choking it. Prisons breed prisons, workhouses workhouses,

[6] "The Emerson-Thoreau Correspondence," *The Atlantic Monthly*, LXIX (1892), p. 745; *Journals and Notebooks*, X, 221, 300.

Army, Government, Church all have their pauperism and
the means of remedy directly are found to have theirs.[7]

The remarkable thing about this journal passage is the extent of
its fatalism. Emerson's more characteristic thought was that the
reform impulse could animate the machine, provide spiritual
vision. But here the "means of remedy" are prone to the same
malfunction; social engineers are necessarily a part of the machine themselves. A few pages later Emerson comments further
on the enclosure of the British mind by describing the "patent
lustre" that "Birmingham" puts on all the nation's products.[8] He
believes England's potentiality both for reform and for cultural
achievement to be adversely affected by the "machine" its own
power has produced.

This image of England as an imprisoning technological society constituted only one element, of course, in the analysis of
national character that Emerson offered in *English Traits*. My
purpose here, however, is not to describe the broader assess-
ment, but to trace the ramifications of this one strain of thought
throughout Emerson's reflections on society in the 1850s.
"Emerson on England" is too often taken as an anomalous subject within his total development: Philip Nicoloff analyzes the
subject insightfully, but he does not make it his business to integrate that analysis into a wider view of Emerson; whereas general students of Emerson—Whicher, Paul, Bishop, Anderson—
quite literally do not mention this aspect of his work. I believe
that the image of technological England remained with Emerson
and provided an essential element in the last major formulation
of his thought.

Emerson himself never thought of England as a topic unre-

[7] *Letters*, III, 452–453; *Journals and Notebooks*, X, 258–59.
[8] *Journals and Notebooks*, X, 260.

lated to other concerns. In fact while still in England in 1848 he began already to assimilate his responses into a broader social analysis, composing for English audiences a new lecture called "The Spirit of the Times." The title should suggest his central question in this lecture: do the Times in fact have a spirit, a spiritual capacity, bent as they are upon material accomplishment? His age would be known, he said, for its devotion to commerce, to tools, and to natural science. And his message about "tools" drew immediately from his observations in Birmingham and Manchester: "Mechanism mechanizes." Just a few months earlier he had called for a "moral engineer" like George Stephenson. Now he repeated the phrase, but used it as illustration of the "very natural but somewhat alarming extension of this age of tools into the social relations." Such engineers wish to "employ men with the same precision and despotism with which they have used shovels and wheels." The mathematical minds of the socialists, he went on, try to apply a "vast arithmetic to society" and turn it into one large machine, a phalanstery. And what they urge on society is coming to pass without their help, because "the large cities are phalansteries." [9] Speaking to an English audience, Emerson was already converting English experience into metaphor for a modern tendency that, by implication, encompassed his own nation as well.

For the two winters after his return to America, Emerson continued to reflect upon this kind of mechanized society in both of his major lecture series, one called "England" and the other, again, "The Spirit of the Times." [10] Meanwhile, as he began to rework his notes on England into a book, his vocabulary for this kind of social limitation increased. It was about

[9] Houghton Library lecture ms., 200 (8), leaves 20, 36.
[10] William Charvat, *Emerson's American Lecture Engagements: A Chronological List* (New York, 1961).

1852 that he first characterized the English as "factitious" and declared as a general principle that "Birmingham birminghamizes all." "Political economy" joined "phalanstery" as a metaphor for the totally engineered society. And by the time that he composed *English Traits* in the middle of the decade, Emerson was capable of remarkably compressed and eloquent statements of his theme:

> Man in England submits to be a product of political economy. On a bleak moor a mill is built, a banking house is opened, and men come in as water in a sluice-way, and towns and cities rise. Man is made as a Birmingham button.[11]

Here Emerson portrays the circumstances of modern England as a condition before which man is passive, a condition which could "make" him rather than dissolve into a self-made universe. Emerson still holds out the possibility that an individual consciousness can, as he put it in a letter from England, "outweigh all Birmingham."[12] The remedy to tyrannous circumstances remains the same: individual assertion of visionary power. But the terms of this assertion have indeed changed. One cannot become a transparent eyeball in Birmingham as easily as on a bare common. The individual consciousness must move mountains, must outweigh Birmingham, in order to be self-reliant. Such metaphors of oppression and engulfment suggest a new kind of conflict for the soul, a conflict at least potentially tragic.

This sense of spiritual obstruction reached its most forceful statement, however, not in *English Traits* but in Emerson's most remarkable late essay, "Fate," the first essay in *The Conduct of Life.* "In our first steps to gain our wishes," Emerson wrote

[11] *Journals and Notebooks,* X, 501; *Works,* V, 98.
[12] *Letters,* III, 455.

there, "we come upon immovable limitations," upon "laws of
the world." [13] "Fate" was in fact Emerson's most characteristic
idea throughout the fifties, beginning as a lecture title in 1851
and reaching published form in 1860. As such, it was closely in-
terwoven with his reflections on English and American society;
in fact Emerson thought out both subjects in the same few
years, especially in the year he described himself as Pythagoras,
1851. As a result of this interweaving, Fate became among other
things a crucial tool of *social* analysis for Emerson. It was the ge-
neric term for the social limitation that Emerson had first perceived as Birmingham. Let me point out the growth of this idea
in some detail.

Emerson began reflecting on the cosmic principle "Fate" as
he read Oriental literature during the forties, and to him the
word meant particularly the defeat of character by earthly circumstance. "It is a sign of our impotence and that we are not yet
ourselves." [14] The circumstances he had in mind were often biological; especially after the English trip and in response to contact with English scientists, the journals were filled with reflections about the limits placed on the freedom of men and animals
by nature. His fatalism was never absolute. The scientists had
also suggested a process by which nature itself overcame Fate:
Emerson began reflecting on evolution as the means by which
material circumstances constantly transcended their own limitations. [15] Evolution, Emerson believed, was the principle that in-
sured ultimate victory of character over circumstance. The word
Fate itself, however, was shorthand for his most pessimistic
series of thoughts.

Fate did not suggest oppressing *social* circumstances to

[13] *Works*, VI, 3–4.   [14] *Journals and Notebooks*, VIII, 228.
[15] See *Journals*, VIII, 8–9, 16, 50–51, etc.

Emerson until early in the 1850s. I have not found any use of
the term in his writing from the late forties about machine-like
England. The concepts of Fate and of social mechanization seem
to have had their beginning in separate, though parallel, reflections. Soon, however, Emerson did begin to analyze social situa-
tions from the perspective of Fate. He did so first in response to
American rather than English events. What I take to be a crucial
equation occurs in his journal in 1850: "*The Times.* That is to
say, there is Fate; Laws of the world; what then?" The Times,
the social circumstances in which one lives, are now perceived as
a product of the same tyranny that governs the animal. And
"the Times" that spring meant one thing to Emerson: the failure
of spiritual values in America revealed in the passage of the
Fugitive Slave Law. Men, he concluded, have no opinions, no
virtue, no sense of principle higher than expediency; "the
badness of the Times is making death attractive." [16] Emerson
saw the Times as a force, like Fate and like Birmingham, spell-
ing death to the soul unless it was willing to struggle. The Fugitive Slave crisis, and the fatalistic materialism it revealed, op-
pressed Emerson as the more distant circumstances of England
could not have.

But all of these images of resistance—naturalistic Fate, English machine, godless Times—came to bear upon each other in
1851. The journals for this year include entries pages long on
two subjects, the limitations of Fate and the immorality of political compromise. Meanwhile, important lectures took shape.
The year started with Emerson giving isolated lectures from the
series that would be called "The Conduct of Life"; and then, in
March, he gave the whole series under that title in Pittsburgh.
Interestingly enough, though, the first lecture in the series was
not "Fate." The ideas for that were still being worked out in

[16] *Journals*, VIII, 88, 112.

journal form. Instead the series began with his three-year-old lecture "England." Discussion of England must have served as a declaration of the material laws of the world. From this he could move on, in order, to "Laws of Success," "Wealth," "Economy"—and then ascending the scale of values, "Culture" and "Worship." [17] Nowhere is there better evidence of the parallel between these two metaphors for the world's realities; both England and Fate serve to represent what tyrannizes the passive self and converts to power for the visionary self.

A month after this series was completed, Emerson gave the most enraged and most partisan address of his career, "The Fugitive Slave Law," to the residents of Concord. Again he spoke in terms of a weight falling upon the individual self, but this time the ascent to victory was less certain than in the lecture series. An "ignominy" has fallen over Massachusetts, he proclaimed, an "infamy" is in the air, which "has forced us all into politics." Like Pythagoras as described two months later, Emerson felt both the necessity of descending into this realm and the pain, the struggle, of doing so. It is here for the first time that Emerson enunciated his own rationale for civil disobedience; and we feel the personal effort of the choice for him in his likening of action against slavery to digging away a mountain of sorrow. Emerson also used images of weight, enclosure, and degradation to characterize Daniel Webster's compromise of principle for material good in supporting the Fugitive Slave Law. "All the drops of his blood have eyes that look downward." In Webster's obedience to a "powerful animal nature," Emerson said in his journal, "Fate has been too strong for him." [18]

The rather desperate hope of the address was that Fate and animal nature would not prove equally strong to Emerson him-

[17] Charvat, p. 26.
[18] *Works*, XI, 179, 209, 204; *Journals*, VIII, 231.

self and to Massachusetts. "We are examples of Fate," he wrote
that summer. "Toss up a pebble and it falls. And the soaring of
your mind and the magnanimity you indulge will fall. But cannot we ride the horse that now throws us?" [19] Again the possibility of victory is held out here, the possibility of converting
conditions that oppress into enabling circumstances. But only
through resistance—this time by training wild horses. The
problem is suggested by the title of the lectures: "The *Conduct* of
Life." "Conduct" suggests temporal duration, not momentary
soaring; and it implies the need to steer a path through difficulties. When Emerson repeated this series in December of 1851,
beginning now with the lecture "Fate," [20] he did affirm the possibility of conducting life through Fate to Freedom. But the
unique emphasis of this address fell on the need to overcome obstacles prior to such a victory. Emerson's awareness of these obstacles, both personal and social, had certainly coalesced in the
course of the year.

The concerns of 1851 could be taken as a microcosm for the
whole decade. In a period when Emerson's most characteristic
thoughts were the manifestations and the means of overcoming
Fate, his focused topic of study was the nature of English and
American society. I have tried to show here how cross-fertiliza-
tion took place in one way between these concerns during the
first year or two of the 1850s: lecturing frequently on technological England and reflecting on slave-holding America, Emerson
began to think of society itself as a manifestation of Fate. But I
have also said that Fate in turn became a useful tool of social
analysis. If this is so, we might expect Emerson to put the concept to work explicitly in his comparative analysis of England
and America during the years that followed. And in fact he did

[19] *Journals*, VIII, 239.   [20] Charvat, p. 26.

just this, asking of each society whether the material circumstances of nature and technology would entrap it or provide power for intellectual and spiritual accomplishment.

In *English Traits* Emerson concluded tactfully but firmly that the British nation had become a victim of Fate. The word Fate emerges in the journal passages about England that Emerson started recording about 1852 in preparation for his book, and it is linked immediately to the metaphors of mechanistic limitation already worked out in his mind. "What Englishman," Emerson asked in 1853, "has idealism enough to lift the horizon of brass which shuts down like an umbrella close around his body?" This horizon of brass, he concluded, illustrates "the power of Fate, the dynastic oppression of submind." [21] In *English Traits* England's wealth is seen as a product of this same "submind" in that it has never taken "the step beyond" its own sufficiency either to remedy the wrongs it has produced or to create a genuine culture. Both in its capacity for social management and in the life of the mind, Emerson concluded, England "is in the stream of Fate, one victim more in the common catastrophe." It would be possible to view Emerson's celebration of Saxon racial strength as a case study in positive, productive response to Fate, to biological and geographical determinism. But this perspective condemns England's present condition all the more. Even Carlyle, with whom Emerson visits Stonehenge and Winchester, scenes of past Saxon achievement, has been "driven by his disgust at the pettiness and the cant into the preaching of Fate." At Winchester the two men read that the body of Alfred—whom Emerson had earlier extolled as "the type of the race"—now lies covered by modern buildings and by ruins of the old. Again the individual is literally buried by a

[21] *Journals*, VIII, 239.

mountain of oppressions. England, Emerson asserted in his chapter on "Literature," has become "a roaring volcano of Fate." [22] England represented to him a society thoroughly imprisoned by "the laws of the world," a society where the individual soul is impotent.

His view of America's relation to Fate was more complex. There was a strong nationalistic aspect to this analysis; Emerson wished to assert that the good of England was now in America and would thrive without the calamities visited upon the parent nation. This is the Emerson speaking at the end of *English Traits*, telling Carlyle at Stonehenge about the fanatic dreams still possible on his own "great sloven continent," telling his bourgeois hosts in Manchester that if they do not solve their crises there will still be "elasticity and hope" for mankind on the Allegheny ranges. [23] This Emerson is also evident in his lecture "The Anglo-American," given many times in the years from 1853 to 1855 and in effect a final chapter to *English Traits* not included in the published book. "Anglo-American" reflects Emerson's experiences in the early fifties lecturing west of the Alleghenies and along the Mississippi River. And on the Mississippi Fate was crude natural power—not Birmingham, not a horizon of brass. There, he said, men "followed the river" quite literally; their lives assumed its gigantic form. There "the American . . . appears passively to yield to this superincumbent Fate. His task is to educe the capabilities of the continent, to make the most of it." Emerson's faith in evolution as growth out of material circumstances reaches one of its strongest formulations here. Fate, it would seem, is on the side of America; it leads directly, Emerson asserted in one of his most imperialistic statements, to "the natural growth of the republic." [24]

[22] *Works*, V, 169, 170, 249, 290, 255.   [23] *Works*, V, 314.
[24] Houghton Library lecture ms., 202 (2), leaves 24, 42, 46.

But if we conclude that Emerson is entirely an apologist for imperial America, we are reckoning without the allusions to Fate during those same years in which he characterizes a materialistic and slaveholding society's moral bankruptcy. When he spoke of these matters, America fared no better than England. If Emerson saw English society as a mill that Birminghamized men, he observed in his second address on the Fugitive Slave Law that American slavery was a mill for turning men into monkeys.[25] The machine that symbolized England's death was at work in America too. Even the natural power of the American West Emerson could affirm only if men used it to advance beyond material good to moral affirmation. And he saw a new kind of materialism taking over in America: not the metallic precision of Birmingham, but the "counterfeit" of mindless growth. America, he said even in the optimistic "Anglo-American" lecture, had so far built only "shingle palaces." [26] Emerson the advocate of American growth was always chastened by Emerson the critic of whatever was shoddy, immoral, or self-serving. In the long run he knew that Fate could catch up with America as it had with England.

It was in the published book *Conduct of Life* that Emerson interpreted the relationship of England and America to Fate most broadly; he assimilated his description of England's limitation and America's potential into more general possibilities open to individuals in both societies. He no longer tried at all to exempt America from the more tyrannous aspects of Fate. The essay "Fate" begins with the problem of "The Times," and Emerson speaks of articles on the subject in both Boston and London journals. Indeed he seems to be addressing his whole Anglo-American audience, an audience coping with shared

[25] *Works*, XI, 227.
[26] Houghton Library lecture ms., 202 (2), leaf 12.

modern experience. Instead of speaking about the "mill" of English industrialism or the "mill" of American slavery, he characterizes Fate, "the terms by which our lives are walled up," as possessing "the mechanical exactness . . . of a loom or mill." Emerson has brought Birmingham home to America by recharacterizing it as Fate. The distrust of spiritual values resulting from such a mill, Emerson implies in "Worship," manifests itself equally on both sides of the Atlantic. The English suspected Cobden was advocating free trade for his own profit, and American slavery propagandists have tried to make the idea of "higher law" a laughing matter. Finally, the kind of obedience to Fate that Emerson had attributed to the western American, the obedience that offers a means of getting beyond it to Freedom, is also presented now as a possibility in either nation. Stephenson proved himself to be England's best engineer, Emerson says, by laying out his railroad alongside a river, whereas his colleague Brunel wanted to go in a straight line from city to city.[27] "Following the river," following the necessities of nature, becomes a means of transforming potential tyranny into power for any modern man of vision.

What resulted from Emerson's encounter with England and Fate in this last decade before the Civil War, then, was the first substantial American study of a culture formed by modern technological power. If the primary source of insight into such a technological world was England, the resulting focus of insight included America. And this, I would like to suggest, was a remarkable achievement on Emerson's part. Industrial England had stood facing America for many decades, but Americans were slow to apply its lessons to themselves. If on the one hand they approached England with Irving's Anglophile reverence, as

[27] *Works*, VI, 19, 209–11, 121–22.

the masses of travel writers did, they managed quite well to pre-
tend that Manchester and Birmingham did not exist at all. The
England that mattered lay elsewhere. And if on the other hand
they wrote nationalistic attacks on England, in the tradition of
the *Inichquin* controversy, they seized upon the troubles of industrial England only as fault-finders; their basic rationale was
to locate themselves in opposition to the world observed. Both
American sensibilities presented obstacles to a self-implicating
analysis of England's machine-made society.

The nationalistic impulse was strong in Emerson, of course,
and in much of his Anglo-American writing it prevails. But on
the deeper level, where experience was assimilated into primary
concept and metaphor, his pessimistic reflections about England
informed a larger view of man and society. He was, after all, no
polemicist in his defense of America, but a student of all human
consciousness. England might provide a continuing metaphor
for the entrapment of men in society's mechanical structures;
but while the place could serve to represent a human condition,
the condition did not have to exist only and literally in that
place.

A few contemporary American writers did approach England with an equally complex and probing imagination. Cooper
certainly combined nationalistic fault-finding with a desire to
analyze America's own deficiencies. But the world of "Birmingham," of modern city and technology, was far from his
mind; very much a child of the eighteenth century, he analyzed
the implications of aristocratic privilege and did not enter upon
the ground which so interested Emerson. Hawthorne was closer
to Emerson both in time and in preoccupation. He spent four
years during the 1850s as a resident of Liverpool, and his *English
Notebooks* include, if not any thoughts about the mechanism of
industrial England, long and indignant descriptions of the Liver-

pool poor. But his central impulse was that of the Anglophile: to find his own "old home" in picturesque England. And that was the central theme of his writing about England both in the essays called *Our Old Home* and in the abortive romance *Dr. Grimshawe's Secret*. Hawthorne always sought for a fictional pattern that would allow for both reverential and critical description of England from an American's perspective, but he never found one. His "Outside Glimpses of English Poverty" never led anywhere, as Emerson's encounter with Birmingham did.

Only one of Emerson's American contemporaries pursued the implications of English technology as far, and that was Melville, the Melville of *Redburn* and *Israel Potter*. In *Israel Potter*, published just a year before *English Traits*, Melville too portrayed a modern life enclosed and crippled by mechanistic society, he too associated such enclosure with life in England, and he too explored the relationship between this England and his own America. The differences are, of course, striking. Melville focused on the American nationalistic theme by making his hero a Revolutionary War soldier, and he did so in order to deflate such nationalism. His method was that of an ironist: after depicting an American hero trapped in an England rendered satanic by war, technology and poverty, he brought Israel Potter back home not to freedom, but to near-collision with a patriotic wagon careening through the streets of Boston. American nationalism itself takes on the relentless mechanical qualities of England. And, of course, Israel Potter's defeat is total: certainly no means of transcending "Fate" is offered him. Now Emerson did not share either this sense of ironic discrepancy or this tragic vision. He brought Birmingham home to America by assimilation, not by deflation of myth; and he reconciled it to growth and evolution, seeing transcendence rather than defeat as a possible end to the struggle. But the two writers stood on common ground in their sense of what the obstacles to a full human life might be. We are used to thinking of Emerson as a man with a deficient sense of evil, and Melville—most of all, perhaps, Melville in *Israel Potter*—as a man nearly paralyzed by his awareness of suffering. But these two documents of the 1850s share both a sense of the individual's struggle against deadening mechanization and an explicit denial of America's exemption from that struggle. No other American writer equally felt the impact of the mechanized English world upon his own until Henry Adams wrote about his trip through the Black District.

To make such a claim assumes the possibility of taking Emerson's social insights seriously, and indeed I wish to do so. Throughout his career, but especially in this decade of considering the Conduct of Life in a modern Anglo-American culture, social questions enter significantly into his dialectic of soul and world. Images of society can occur on either side of this dialectic: they can represent either an expanded identity for the soul or a barrier to the soul's assertion. I have been emphasizing barriers here: Pythagoras' sea of wreckage, the Times, Birmingham, the mill, Fate all represent the world of "not me," the world into which the self is incarnated or against which the self contends. The recognition of these counterforces to self-reliance itself constitutes an important kind of social vision, because it makes necessary an engagement of the individual self in its surrounding world.

In addition, however, Emerson's contention with Fate led him to consider society in another sense, that is, on the other side of the dialectic. It is not always the individual soul that must outweigh Birmingham or navigate its sea of troubles; Emerson increasingly makes room for a collective cultural enterprise of resistance to materialism. *English Traits* and "The Anglo-American" are centrally occupied with questions of total cultural vitality; and in *The Conduct of Life* Emerson speaks again and again of cultural questions despite his opening admission that he is "incompetent to solve the times." "Worship," the crucial essay in the book in terms of transition from Fate to Freedom, ends with the vision not of a new man, but of a "new church" for the society as a whole, a culturally shared sense of spirituality.[28]

Emerson aimed for the "melioration" or evolutionary growth of the society as a whole, but increasingly in the 1850s he recognized the role of a minority culture in affecting the direction of the whole. In *English Traits* he wrote that if the British still contained "retrieving power" it lay among a "minority of profound minds" which, though vastly outweighed, might by its discord yield new power. This minority constituted one of "two nations" in England, a class of perception and genius alongside a larger, materially oriented class.[29]

In this sense America too contained "two nations." The same year that he was working out this idea about the English, Emerson spoke on his favorite subject, the scholar in America, to the students of Williams College. His address offers a good indication of the distance he had come since he first described the "American Scholar" to Harvard students in 1837. At that time "Man Thinking" was to be a complete individual, "self-relying and self-directed." In 1854 Emerson proclaimed that "the Scholars are an organic caste or class" in an "Anglo-Saxon society" resembling "a great industrial corporation." The society in which scholars dwell, in other words, is a mechanistic and fatalistic Birmingham, a society immersed, Emerson said, in a "vulgarity" which "came to us, with commerce, out of England." Here is a fine example of Emerson's perception in the

[28] *Works*, VI, 3, 241.   [29] *Works*, V, 259.

mid-1850s of society as an oppressive collectivity. But resistance is not simply his own personal business. The scholars, he went on to assert, are "accountable for this materialism"; they as another collectivity must understand it and resist its tyranny.[30] The obstructions set in the way of the scholar by modern Anglo-Saxon society demand engagement both of the individual and of the class.

Emerson has perhaps seemed aloof from social questions partly because he refused to be a reformer in an age of reform; he never followed the Abolitionists in America or Carlyle in England in their direct proposal of remedies for perceived ills. But his concern for a society's capacity to encourage the full development of the human soul involves, after all, the question of culture in its broadest sense—the question of an Arnold much more than a Carlyle. And indeed his appeal for a class of scholars or a new church does point toward the issues that Arnold would make central a decade later in *Culture and Anarchy*. The similarities are strong: Arnold portrayed a majority culture beset with the danger of too much "faith in machinery," in wealth and in mere bodily prosperity; he argued that a minority of men professing different values—the Oxford movement, for instance—could create new currents of life and feeling in a society despite short-term defeat; and he concluded that such apparent elitists were indeed "the true apostles of equality," because they worked for the creation of a genuine *national* vitality and intelligence. But I don't wish to move Emerson from his own center and convert him into a Victorian critic of culture. The issues of cultural materialism and idealism, of majority and minority values, are surely present in his thought, but they are present as corollaries to the central drama of individual vision. Arnold argued that

[30] *Journals*, VIII, 471–73.

"perfection . . . is not possible while the individual remains isolated"; he saw the end of culture as the creation of a *communal* "perfect man." Even in his passage about the "new church," on the other hand, Emerson characterized it as a form of worship which "shall send man home to his central solitude." Even in his description of an American scholar accountable for the nation's materialism, he went on from such "secular and outward benefit" to the quality of the individual's own soul.

What we have here, then, is not Arnold's cultural criticism any more than it is Melville's tragic portrayal of a man's destruction. It is, as ever with Emerson, an essentially affirmative vision of the individual's emergence into full consciousness. But it is an affirmative vision that takes fully into account the difficulties and responsibilities of existence in a modern technological society. This society provides both the world in which the soul must necessarily exist as it reaches for vision, and a significant object of the soul's action or vocation once vision has been reached. "Melioration" of the whole society will take place only through the "incarnation" of many individuals.

In fact personal vocation in a Birminghamized world cannot always *proceed from* vision; much more often Man Thinking must work on an ambiguous middle ground that partakes of both matter and spirit, Fate and Freedom, uncertain at any given moment what the results will be. Thus on the one hand the sense of struggle and obstruction is often dominant. But on the other, the possibility of imminent transformation is there too, the possibility that the actual conditions of Fate might produce power. The water that drowns one man, Emerson says, buoys up the other who knows how to swim; an iron bar that seems an obstacle can become a conductor. The point is, though, that the individual or society engaged in this process of transformation feels no assurance of victory. One is asked to exercise an attitude of trust and acceptance rather than require fully adequate forms of vision and action in the present.

This balance between a sense of limitation and a promise of fulfillment best characterizes Emerson's later thinking on his relation to the Times. Though the conditions of Fate and the Times are often perceived in adversarial terms, as a beast or a machine to conquer, they can also of themselves become a means to vision. Emerson ends *The Conduct of Life* not with Pythagoras still floundering in his sea, but with the story of Thor, who was set three tasks to do and only later found that he had been drinking the sea, and wrestling Time, and racing Thought. Almost parodying his earlier and more lofty Transcendentalist, Emerson imagines us demanding, " 'Set me some great task, ye gods! and I will show my spirit.' " But we are required instead to contend with "seeming trifles," with "bad company and squalid conditions." And he concludes, "If we weave a yard of tape in all humility, and as well as we can, long hereafter we shall see that it was no cotton tape at all, but some galaxy which we braided, and that the threads were Time and Nature." [31] It is this need to "work and affirm" that is Emerson's final response to the obstacles he perceives as Fate. He presents the need for such affirmation both to the individual soul and to a modern Anglo-American culture seeking for faith and value amidst its own materialism.

[31] *Works*, VI, 320–21.

Maurice Gonnaud

EMERSON AND THE IMPERIAL SELF:

A EUROPEAN CRITIQUE

AMONG THE SWEEPING though perceptive judgments scattered about Tocqueville's *Democracy in America* is the notion that the Americans, like the French but unlike the English, are given to intellectual generalizations. They need to discover common rules in all things, Tocqueville claims, and to explain a broad constellation of facts by reference to one cause. Recent literary criticism in America must be very American indeed, if one considers the wealth of studies which purport to subsume wide arrays of works, writers, or attitudes under common descriptions. One of the latest in date, Professor Quentin Anderson's *The Imperial Self*, is also one of the most ambitious. With unfaltering single-mindedness, it attempts to identify an original current running through American literature from Emerson to Henry Miller and Allen Ginsberg, and affecting such diverse, and apparently incommensurable, figures as Whitman and Henry James. The best summary of the book's overall theme occurs in the preface; "I believe," Professor Anderson writes, "that the habit scholars have of calling Emerson misty or abstract, calling Whitman a successful charlatan, calling Henry James ambiguous, are but ways of referring to an inchoate perception of the absolutism of the self. . . . This absolutism involves an extreme passivity, which is complemented by, *must* be complemented by, the claim of the imperial self to mastery of what has almost overwhelmed it." [1]

The author's vision of his subject could hardly be put with more neatness. However, the treatment, as a European (and a Frenchman at that!) sees it, fails to come up to the standard of cogent clarity established in the preface. For one thing, the argument is both repetitive and circuitous; it develops, one would say, on the assumption that rhapsodizing insistence fits the situation better than logical progression. Then the tone is wilfully idiosyncratic, with oblique cryptical comments or references involving the foreign reader in sudden obscurity. The effect at times is reminiscent of that produced by such blatantly American works as *The Education of Henry Adams* or William Carlos Williams' *Paterson*, in which full perception of the meanings intended depends on an intimate knowledge not only of the particulars but of the minutiae of the author's cultural context.

On second thought, however, most of these strictures fall away or reveal an aptness to be turned upside down: instead of confusing the issue, they become an index of the critic's thorough comprehension of the implications of his subject. By roaming over the wide field he has circumscribed in almost impertinent freedom, by ignoring the demands of flat social communication, by spurning linear constructions and throwing out at climactic moments hints which challenge the reader to a reexamination of his own views, Professor Anderson shows the self-assurance of an imperial self. There is in the last analysis a deep congruity between the thesis of the book, and the method, combining casualness with insight, by which the author en-

[1] Quentin Anderson, *The Imperial Self, An Essay in American Literary and Cultural History* (New York, 1971), pp. ix–x.

deavors to suggest both its central relevance to an understanding of American literature, and its stubborn elusiveness.

While it would be excessive to greet *The Imperial Self* as a totally fresh approach to the subject (I was often reminded, when reading it, of Professor Richard Poirier's pioneering study, *A World Elsewhere*), Professor Anderson's book focuses with particular brilliance on what constitutes for a European, and especially for a Frenchman, the distinctive, and not a little puzzling, core of American literature. I have tried in vain to locate in our own tradition a similar current that would bear comparison with the cumulative, organically connected achievement of Emerson, Whitman and James. At best one thinks of dazzling but peripheral figures like Lautréamont, Rimbaud or, at the other cultural extremity, Mallarmé. Nor is the reason for this lack of symmetry very hard to find. The mode illustrated in their several ways by Emerson, Whitman, and James derives much of its vitality from the persistence, or from the resurgence under kindred forms, of the spirit of Protestantism. It owes a great deal, too, to German romanticism and to the philosophical revolution initiated by Kant. But it uncompromisingly rejects all manners of feeling, all habits of thought bred by Catholicism or its political equivalent, an instinctive acceptance of established authority. Emerson's disgust with contemporary Italy, his obstinate disparagement of France and the French character are almost ludicrous examples of the length to which antipathy against a culture felt to be intrinsically alien can be carried. The development of the imperial self follows upon one of those enormous repudiations with which H. G. Wells once credited Stephen Crane. A European like myself can only take note of the fact and do his best to adjust to the consequences.

This is precisely where a book like Professor Anderson's comes in handy to the perplexed foreigner. The task it performs is best understood by reference to a fine page in the concluding chapter, in which he defines the greatness of Perry Miller as historian of American culture, praises his astounding grasp of intellectual complexities and points to some symmetrical limitations. "But what Miller notably lacked," he writes, "was a nose for those qualities in thought and language which reflect the dream state, the kind of perception that Nietzsche had of the oppositions, doublenesses, contradictions and condensations that find their way into systems of thought and into attempts to change them. He was innocent, for example, of what a good many historians of culture now posit without always being explicit about: the psychic need manifested by a particular generation." [2] Professor Anderson's enterprise supplements and to some extent supersedes that of Miller through a deliberate reversal of emphases. The debate over ideas, even in their dramatic function of testing experience and extending its range, is pushed into the background, while the emotional forces at work behind verbal expression, the resulting distribution of energy between the self and the outer world and finally the process of validation of language operating in the void of consciousness become the author's primary concern. Confining the scope of this paper to a discussion of the imperial self in the context of Emerson's work (and this is, no doubt, a severe restriction to the author's own understanding of his subject), I would say that Professor Anderson invites us simultaneously to measure the efficacy of Emerson's language and to realize the loss sustained in the course of expression. The writings themselves are ultimately of interest only in so far as they capture, channel, and radiate out in absorbable form significant amounts of psychic energy.

It is clear that such an approach, as Professor Anderson

[2] *Imperial Self*, pp. 231–32.

himself is anxious to point out, has been encouraged by the
great revulsion of the 1960s. The loosening of social ties beyond
anything experienced by the United States since their foundation, the revolt against parental authority, the calling into question of all rules, all sanctions not authenticated by the self, un-
dermined the orthodoxies of reason and put a special premium
on language unhampered by proprieties, unworn by usage, ut-
tering as its primary function the deepest fantasies of the soul.
As an observer from abroad, however, I find it rather admirable
that Emerson should have been hailed so widely and so fer-
vently at this juncture as the great forerunner of the drive for
total emancipation. This recognition, to my mind, reveals the
literary alertness of the American people, their awareness of
where their true riches lie as well as their ability to interpret
major literary figures in terms of the burning interests of the
day—a procedure amounting to a permanent reactivation of the
nation's cultural heritage which might profitably be adopted by
the Old World. More remarkably still, Emerson's subver-
siveness was identified in its full virulence, despite the thick
coating of antiquarianism wrapped about his language which
deadens the thrust of ideas and deflects many of the reader's ef-
forts to get at the gist of his message. In that sense, Professor
Anderson's working assumption finds itself handsomely corrob-
orated: there is a liveliness about the words used by Emerson
that transcends any formulation narrowly connected with the
fashions of a period.

So far, we have been concerned with a sort of updating of
Emerson based on a recent cultural experience. The scholar's
work begins where Professor Anderson attempts to use for a
clarification of his subject some of the insights vouchsafed to us
by our time. I have in mind here more particularly his remarks
on Unitarianism and his placing of the Jacksonian Republic in a

dialectic relation to that of the Founding Fathers—both fine examples of how imagination propped on serious information and capable of a transfer of sympathy from the present to the past can fill in a gap or correct a usual mistake.

Professor Anderson refuses to endorse Emerson's curt condemnation of the "pale negations" of Unitarianism. He shows instead how the notion, capital to Unitarian thinking, of a man, Jesus, endowed with genuine godly powers, was by itself self-contradictory and radically unstable. He proceeds to illustrate the drift towards a general recognition of the voice of the self by quoting extensively from early numbers of the unexceptionable *Christian Examiner*. Emerson's own career closely parallels that evolution. Only the publication, too long delayed already, of the whole set of his sermons will reveal how secure he felt for the better part of a decade within the pale of the Unitarian Church, and how proportionately unsettling was the discovery that he made in the late 1820s of the inadequacy of his position as a minister. On this head, Professor Henry Nash Smith's article on Emerson's problem of vocation, published over twenty years ago, contains all the necessary observations and has not been superseded. Professor Anderson's personal contribution lies in his tying together the world of religion and the world of politics to establish Emerson's redoubtable predicament in the early 1830s. The passing away of what he calls a society of deference, resting upon an unquestioned hierarchy of functions, coincided with the climax of his spiritual crisis and compounded his sense of bewilderment and loss.

The bold, strategic manoeuvre by which he achieved victory, turning the cramped tottering self of the dismayed minister into a luminous fountain of strength, makes up the argument of a story which has often been told, though, predictably enough, never in such a way as to make that victory seem inevi-

table. Professor Anderson takes over where his predecessors, notably Professors Sherman Paul and Jonathan Bishop, had left
off. Against the interpretations influenced more or less openly
by the methods of the New Criticism, with its disregard of anything but semantics and the verbal relations discoverable within
a given text, Professor Anderson takes what may seem an old-
fashioned stand. To all intents and purposes, he joins hands
with Henry James, who had marvelled at Emerson's faculty for
speaking to the soul "in a voice of direction and authority" in
spite of the formlessness of his manner, and shifts the weight of
"secular incarnation" (Professor Anderson's own phrase) from
the writer and the articulations of language back to the man and
the preacher. But he does not lapse into a repetition of the moral
generalities characteristic of the first school of Emerson criticism
in the 1880s and 1890s. His concern is with the preacher drawing upon the resources of the imperial self in order to awaken
other imperial selves in his audience—with the preacher, that is,
engaged in a truly democratic effort of communication. How the
spell worked, and at what cost to the preacher himself, makes
up the burden of Professor Anderson's analysis.

Emerson felt keenly the obligation put on a living soul to
dilate, so to speak, in the presence of another soul. "Life goes
headlong," he wrote in a Journal entry dated 1842, "each of us is
always to be found hurrying headlong in the chase of some fact,
hunted by some fear or command behind us. Suddenly we meet
a friend. We pause. Our hurry and empressement look ridicu-
lous. Now pause, now possession is required, and the power to
swell the moment from the resources of our own heart until it
supersedes sun and moon and solar system in its expanding immensity." [3] The preacher must work out the same conversion in

[3] *The Journals and Miscellaneous Notebooks of Ralph Waldo Emerson*
(Cambridge, Mass., 1960–   ), VIII (1970), 204.

response to the same unexpressed demand, but success is at best fitful and short-lived. Hence there is a truly Promethean quality to Emerson's utterance, which affirms millennial certainties and falters in its desperate attempt to induce faith in them. At its most ecstatic, the voice palpitates both in and out of the frame of traditional rhetorics. The endless striving for adequate expression, which is Emerson's homage to the ineffable, is itself inseparable from oral cadences overheard on the printed page. Far more could be done in the field of stylistic analysis to elucidate the subtle proportions in which the virtues of the spoken word alternately clash and blend with those of the written one in the finished prose of the *Essays*.

Professor Anderson points the way, at least obliquely, to such explorations, just as he indicates a fruitful path when he makes the remark that abstraction is the most poetic vehicle at Emerson's command, because it is also the most universal, the most pregnant with unspent possibilities. It is interesting to observe that the distinction implicitly made here between an upstream language, preceding the fragmenting process of experience, and a downstream language, concerned with the products of fragmentation, anticipates the crucial metaphor of the cataract splitting into an infinity of separate drops, which underlies William Carlos Williams' poem, *Paterson*. The American imagination seems indeed to have been obsessed with a sense of the fall, or the degradation, inherent in any action, any accomplishment. Its natural atmosphere is the light of early dawn, when dissolving darkness begets a world swollen with the promise of objects, but unhurt yet by their angularity. Characteristically, Professor Anderson describes Emerson's effect on the listener or the reader as a deliberate *blurring* of what is nearest at hand and of what is most remote. Who would not agree that the fascination exercised by "The American Scholar" depends to a large extent on the author's ability to suggest this exquisite but precarious moment in time, when virtualities hover over the world of facts in an effortless reconciliation of freedom and power? Professor Anderson is probably right when he claims that, strictly speaking, there is no American romanticism, because of an ingrained aversion for the quiddity of things in the handful of writers who could qualify for inclusion in that all too vague literary family.

There is, however, an aspect of the imperial self which, to my mind, deserves fuller consideration than it receives in Professor Anderson's book. To the extent that it functions as the creator of an autonomous universe, it must seek to disengage itself ever more completely from the pressures, frictions and contingencies of the outer world which might threaten and ultimately destroy its primacy. Not only evil, as Professor Anderson remarks after many others, but the impact of death as a force thwarting the self's impulse towards total harmony is quietly and somewhat shockingly ignored by Emerson. On the very day of his first wife's decease, in February 1831, he wrote to his aunt Mary Moody Emerson, who he knew would sympathize with his feeling: "My angel is gone to heaven this morning, and I am alone in the world and strangely happy." [4] Besides the odd sense of relief experienced, once everything is over, by all those who have had to watch the pangs of coming death, there is in this sentence the confession of positive joy: the link between deprivation and happiness is unmistakable. Likewise, the freezing ideality of the concluding section of the essay on Friendship stems from an ill-suppressed yearning to move in a final leap beyond the reach of human entanglement. The paradox, already noted by Professor Poirier, is that visionary possession coincides with utter relinquishment. No compromise is possible, since the

---

[4] *The Letters of Ralph Waldo Emerson* (New York, 1939), I, 318.

imperial self can secure and reinforce its authority only through further retreat into its own fantasies.

What the stress of sustaining this literally inhuman attitude must have been to Emerson is fairly easy to imagine, though it does not come through with the expected degree of emphasis in Professor Anderson's book. Professor Poirier again, and Norman Brown, who suggests in *Life Against Death* that any person breaking away from a common religious belief is subject to the necessity of creating his own personal neurosis, are much more illuminating here. Absolute separateness had about it the character of potential tragedy, as Stephen Whicher profoundly intimated, and was bound to produce in time either a shattering of the imperial self or a downright fall into madness (Jones Very's doomed career as the normative figure of transcendentalism comes to mind here). Nor was the halfway house of art, hiding its insubstantial nature behind the permanence of form, available to Emerson. Professor Anderson justly notes that two distinct families made up the unworldly tribe that he studies: there were those who pitched for life and its spontaneous flow, and those who pitched for work and the discipline of composition. Emerson was not, like that extreme example of the second category, Henry James, capable of transcending the predicament of his existence by projecting his fantasies into a substitute world of fiction. For better or worse his vocation was to be, in Matthew Arnold's oft-quoted but still fundamentally relevant phrase, "the friend and aider of those who would live in the spirit." With no alternative course open to him (and his moral strength as well as his honesty were tested in this acceptance of a personal limitation), he faced about slowly, reluctantly, and began a long tussle with reality. It seems to me that Professor Anderson fails to comprehend, or at least to render, the full range of Emerson's ambition to conquer the time-ridden plural-ity of experience, when he passes by that complex process of reorientation. Nothing but the absoluteness of his faith and the exorbitant demands it placed on his psyche compelled Emerson, past a certain point, to accept a drastic reorganization of his mental energies.

Interestingly, the rationale of this new attitude is established in a comment on Jacob Boehme, one of Professor Anderson's references in his measurement of Emerson's shortcomings, which suggests how an ideal of intellectual sharpness had come to displace or make obsolete the primacy of all-absorbing consciousness. "I have never had good luck with Boehme before to-day," Emerson wrote in a Journal entry dated approximately 1844, "and now I see that his excellence is in his comprehensiveness, not like Plato in his precision. His propositions are vague, inadequate and straining. It is his aim that is great. He will know not one thing, but all things. He is like those great swaggering country geniuses that come now and then down from New Hampshire to college, and soon demand to learn not Horace and Homer but also Euclid and Spinoza, and Voltaire, and Palladio, and Columbus, and Bonaparte, and Linnaeus." [5] The emphasis here falls squarely on the task of mature validation which can be carried out only by the self-composed scholar. In keeping with his own demand for more light from the intellect, Emerson undertook to probe some of the crucial assumptions of the imperial self. One of them concerns the completeness of man predicated by faith in his infinite nature, and the rebuff inflicted by experience in the form of sex. Viewed in terms of the findings of psychoanalysis, the issue is an important one, and it deserves special attention here because on this point Professor Anderson is demonstrably in the wrong. It is untrue

[5] *Journals and Notebooks*, IX (1971), 106.

that Emerson contented himself with vaguely metaphysical assertions on the subject, and "never made direct war on the emotional meaning of a heterosexual state." [6]

Several entries in the Journal (some of them, it is true, published for the first time in the edition now in progress) show Emerson pondering over the significance of sex and marriage, and trying to think through his principles at whatever cost to his New England sense of propriety. "A highly endowed man with good intellect and good conscience," he wrote in 1842, "is a Man-woman and does not so much need the complement of Woman to his being as another. Hence his relations to the sex are somewhat dislocated and unsatisfactory. He asks in Woman sometimes the Woman, sometimes the Man." [7] A year later, impatience on recalling the shallowness displayed by some of his interlocutors during a conversation on woman's nature prompted him to a pointed reassertion of the same unorthodox view: "Much poor talk concerning woman, which at least had the effect of revealing the true sex of several of the party who usually go disguised in the form of the other sex. Thus Mrs. B. is a man. The finest people marry the two sexes in their own person. Hermaphrodite is then the symbol of the finished soul." [8] More often, however, a newly-won recognition of the obdurate limits of man qualifies his faith and induces a mood of uneasy skepticism, as in this extract, dated 1841, which I will take the liberty of quoting at some length because of a revealing alternation between the practical and the ideal, each mode coming up on top in the author's mind before subsiding again, as though the fervidly desired reconciliation were forever out of the question:

---

[6] *Imperial Self*, p. 48.   [7] *Journals and Notebooks*, VIII, 175.
[8] *Journals and Notebooks*, VIII, 380.

We cannot rectify marriage because it would introduce such a carnage into our social relations, and it seems the most rabid radical is a good Whig in relation to the theory of Marriage. Yet perhaps we can see how the facts stand in heaven. Woman hides her form from the eyes of men in our world: they cannot, she rightly thinks, be trusted. In a right state the love of one, which each man carried in his heart, should protect all women from his eyes as by the impenetrable veil of indifferency. The love of one should make him indifferent to all others, or rather their protector and saintly friend, as if for her sake. But now there is in the eyes of all men a certain evil light, a vague desire which attaches them to the forms of many women, whilst their affections fasten on some one. Their natural eye is not fixed into coincidence with their spiritual eye. Therefore it will not do to abrogate the laws which make Marriage a relation for life, fit or unfit. Plainly marriage should be a temporary relation, it should have its natural birth, climax and decay, without violence of any kind,—violence to bind or violence to rend. When each of two souls had exhausted the other of that good which each held for the other, they should part in the same peace in which they met, not parting from each other, but drawn to new society. The new love is a balm to prevent a wound from forming where the old love was detached. But now we would not trust even saints and sages with a boundless liberty. For the romance of new love is so delicious that their unfixed fancies would betray them, and they would allow themselves to confound a whim with an instinct, the pleasures of the fancy with the dictates of the character.[9]

When in the lecture "New England Reformers" we see Emerson brushing away the issue with a brief "our marriage is no worse

[9] *Journals and Notebooks*, VIII, 95.

than our education, our diet, our trade, our social custom," [10]
we know better than to take his words as the sign of an all too
easy compliance with accepted forms. From the soul-searching
quality of many entries in the Journal, we can gauge the expen-
diture in moral and intellectual energy which had been necessary to produce the assurance reflected in the simplicity of the
statement.

Another dichotomy, no less disturbing than the one just
mentioned and no less relevant to Professor Anderson's categories advanced for his definition of the imperial self, opposes the
claims of agency to those of spiritual reception, or "incorpo-
ration," to use his terminology. More precisely the question that
Emerson felt he could not evade any longer was whether the
preacher, or the scholar-preacher, can perform his exhortative
function aiming at the communication of spiritual power without the support of personal action. The preoccupation with ef-
fective behavior grows steadily and becomes overwhelming in
the Journal between 1842 and 1845. It directs Emerson's attention over and over again towards the quiet ability of Edmund
Hosmer, his farmer neighbor at Concord, to domesticate nature.
It arouses in him a feeling of passionate admiration for the political talent of Daniel Webster, and dictates his choice of Napoleon
as the first of his representative men. But the years between
1842 and 1845 are also the period when his faith in the infini-
tude of the solitary intellect received considerable reinforcement
from his readings in Oriental Scriptures, especially in the "sublime ethics" of the *Vishnu Purana*. The Journal, as usual, regis-
tered the conflicting pull with complete honesty, not even trying
to shelter Emerson's public role from the consequences. With
the gap between the two orders of reality yawning ever more

[10] *The Complete Works of Ralph Waldo Emerson* (Boston and New
York, Centenary Edition, 1903), III, 262.

widely, the scholar must remain faithful to his vision while accepting all the hazards of misunderstanding and impotent communication. The discomfort of this position is vividly described in an entry dated 1845, in which the ups and downs of persuasion and distrust, self-doubt and self-confidence develop dramatically, leaving the outcome uncertain until the ascent of one more step up the stairway of surprise restores his authority to its original fullness.

> The scholar blunders along on his own path for a time, assured by the surprise and joy of those to whom he first communicates his results; then new solitudes, new marches; but after a time on looking up, he finds the sympathy gone or changed, he fancies himself accused by all the bystanders; the faces of his friends are shaded by grief; and yet no tongue ever speaks of the cause. There is some indictment out against him, on which he is arraigned in many counts, and he cannot learn the charge. A prodigious power we have of begetting false expectations. These are the mistakes of others' subjectiveness. The true scholar will not heed them: jump into another bush, and scratch your eyes in again. He passes on to acquit himself of their charges by developments as surprising as was his first word, by indirections and wonderful *alibis* which dissipate the whole crimination.[11]

I am well aware that I am only repeating or paraphrasing some of Emerson's own statements in the second series of his *Essays* or in the early chapters of *The Conduct of Life*, but I am concerned here with the tone and reserved power rather than with the semantic contents of those statements. The greatness of an essay like "Experience" lies, I suggest, in our sense of the author's being engaged in a pursuit of truth which has all the characters

[11] *Journals and Notebooks*, IX, 295.

of faith except its faculty of radiating happiness. Contrary to
Professor Anderson's opinion, most of the virtues of the imperial
self—its intensity, its magnetism, its incoercible demand for
absoluteness—continue, I think, well into the skeptical phase,
and account for the revival of interest in Emerson's later writings that our existentially-minded epoch has fostered. The focal
point of his reflection has now shifted to reality, its elusiveness,
its endless ambivalence, and the way we can (or cannot) come to
terms with it. But it would be a mistake to associate acknowledged loss of individual power with resignation. Just as the
resources of the imperial self exceeded its manifestations in language, so there is now an exasperation with the paucity of the
world and the blankness of its surfaces which bursts out in Mel-
villean accents, lashing the imagination to perilous forays into
the unknown, exalting those "raging riders," as he calls them in
the lecture "New England Reformers," "who drive their steeds
so hard in the violence of living to forget its illusion." [12] Despite
the finality of the setbacks suffered, the passion for conquest
remains unabated.

One attribute, however, of the imperial self has undergone
a decisive change. The quality of expansiveness so typical of
Emerson's first book, *Nature*, recognizable both in its inner
movement and in its most striking metaphors, has been shed, to
be replaced by concentration, "the one good in life," as a Journal
entry dated 1846 confidently asserts.[13] The development is natural enough. With the creative role of perception called into
question by the discovery of some fatal flaw in the arrangement
of the universe, the writer must learn to economize and to han-
dle his mind with judicious deliberation, so as to bring it to bear
on reality with the sharpest possible effect. Energized by Emer-

[12] *Works*, III, 274.   [13] *Journals and Notebooks*, IX, 366.

son's undiminished intensity of purpose, the new literary strategy not only avoided the risk of narrowness, but increased the resonance of the experience transcribed, made it at once more immediate and more memorable because of a pungency of statement which was the result of a firmer control over the tools of expression. The whole of the essay "Experience," the larger part of "Nominalist and Realist," the central pages of the portrait of Montaigne in *Representative Men*, the opening chapter, "Fate," in *The Conduct of Life* would illustrate with equal felicity this blending of the sinewy and the spiritual, which only an active residuum of the glories of the imperial self can explain. The majestic abstractions and the intimation of unchanging truth are still there, but a haunting awareness of "the evanescence and lubricity of all objects" [14] presses on the writer's consciousness, balances his impulse to believe with the lessons of skepticism and postpones to an unrealized future the accomplishment of man's destiny. If anything, the range and depth of human experience has been increased. It includes now in tingling companionship the wildest promise and the most humiliating frustration.

Given Professor Anderson's concern with the functioning of the imperial self in a state of utmost purity, he is undoubtedly right when he criticizes Emerson for failing to work out to its logical consequence his opposition to the workaday world. He misses or ignores in Emerson, however, the qualities which he finds particularly attractive and praiseworthy in Hawthorne and the other writers of the transitive school. Emerson was no novelist, but in dramatizing the struggles of the imperial self well beyond the point indicated by Professor Anderson, he discovered a way to honor the demands of the soul without hardening himself in fatal isolation or falling prey to illusion, this master

[14] "Experience," *Works*, III, 49.

word and omnipresent bugbear in his late writings. Lowell's witty characterization of Emerson as Plotinus-Montaigne seems to have led many critics (Professor Anderson among them) to the hasty conclusion that he was all his life the helpless victim of what he once diagnosed as the curse of double consciousness.[15] The mature work of Emerson was designed on the contrary to heal the breach opened by "the Fall of Man"—his startling definition, one will remember, of "the discovery we have made that we exist." [16] Need it be specified that the unity which it strove manfully to encompass was only the poor best that was left after the foundering of the undifferentiated self, and that Emerson knew it was?

Here again, it seems to me that Professor Anderson is a little less than fair to Emerson, when he charges him with intellectual inconsistency. Opposing his treatment of History to that of Berdyaev, characterized by unswerving hostility, he writes in the course of a wholesale attack on his method: "He denounced it [history] and made covert use of it." [17] That history was a huge stumbling-block in the way of the imperial self, Emerson himself never denied. He composed the essay bearing that name to dispose of the objections, and indirectly acknowledged their importance by placing it at the head of the first series. That on the other hand the weakening of the imperial self made the positions defended in the essay less and less tenable is also true, but Emerson was not long coming round to a complete reassessment of his views. The effort of readjustment culminated in a lecture, "The Method of Nature," delivered in August 1841—only one year after the publication of the essay. Stephen Whicher has noted the pivotal nature of that discourse, in which the lessons taught by modern science, especially geology, are integrated

[15] "The Transcendentalist," *Works*, I, 353.
[16] "Experience," *Works*, III, 75.   [17] *Imperial Self*, p. 48.

into the frame of the argument and initiate a momentous move towards a recognition of the creative value of History. In fact, they add a new dimension to it, but smooth away the difficulty by causing the past to recede so dizzyingly beyond all traces of human existence that the distinction between time and time-lessness is all but annihilated. Emerson seems at times to have taken his cue from Professor Anderson himself, and to have pondered his remark that the notion of growth is incompatible with the structures of perception elaborated by the imperial self. He is at great pains to show how Nature, "inexact and bound-less," [18] reconciles ecstasy with process through a redundancy of life throbbing in every creature. But the author's intention is not primarily to justify or to explain. The web of ideas is caught into an immense song of celebration, as he describes the flux of Nature streaming into man and supplying him with ever-renewed vigor. Intellectual perceptions coincide, as they should in an economy originally devised by the imperial self, with a sense of limitless power.

Further along the line, and still under the aegis of history interpreted in terms of recent discoveries—this time in the field of biology—one would come upon the concept of race, whose complex roots in philosophy (ancient or modern) and science Professor Philip Nicoloff has examined with meticulous care in his book, *Emerson on Race and History*. Though it is interesting to learn about the breadth of Emerson's reading, and to discover the continued liveliness of his response to the interests (or the fads) of his contemporaries, the importance taken in his late writings by this somewhat misty and disturbing notion suggests a commitment far exceeding the possible influence of either fash-ion or intellectual curiosity. Perhaps two of the categories used by Professor Anderson in his analysis of the effects aimed at by

[18] *Works*, I, 200.

the preacher, the immediate and the prospective, will be of some help here.

Whoever reads the *Journals* for the 1840s and the 1850s cannot fail to be struck by the growing number of the entries dealing with the United States and the American character. This is the period when Emerson's rounds of lectures took him farther and farther away from home, and brought him into contact with more people than he had ever met. Confronted almost daily with manners and habits which he scrutinized in good Yankee fashion, he came to persuade himself that this variegated show was both exciting and meaningful. The future of the nation could be deciphered from those petty details, in which he was now capable of taking unfeigned delight. In 1843, he commented for himself in the Journal (and the title of Professor Anderson's book adds an amusing flavor to his choice of what is intended as a crucial adverb): "An American is served like a noble in these city hotels; and his individuality is much respected; and he may go imperially along all the highways of iron or of water. I like it very much that in the heart of democracy I find such practical illustration of high theories." [19] At the same time, Emerson's mind was set on larger and more perplexing issues. The political revolution initiated by the election of Jackson to the Presidency had shaken many dogmas, raised many doubts, created many problems which the conflict with Mexico complicated even further. Secretly perturbed by the way in which the nation was forging successfully ahead in complete disregard of moral principles, he felt the need, every now and again, to reassure himself by taking a long look at History and its mysterious double face: "The question of the annexation of Texas," he wrote in his Journal in 1844, "is one of those which look very differently to the centuries and to the years. It is very certain

[19] *Journals and Notebooks*, VIII, 331.

that the strong British race which have now overrun so much of this continent, must also overrun that tract, and Mexico, and Oregon also, and it will in the course of ages be of small import by what particular occasions and methods it was done. It is a secular question. It is quite necessary and true to our New England character that we should consider the question in its local and temporary bearings, and resist the annexation with tooth and nail." [20] Still the difficulty remained and plagued his conscience.

In effect, the concept of national destiny, buttressed as it was for Emerson on scientific findings about race, resolved the contradiction. It turned out to be the unifying factor, articulating the claims of power, morality and universal change, for which he had been groping all along. Each individual found himself vicariously fulfilled in the present and future achievements of his community. This fusion of the immediate and the prospective, to hark back to Professor Anderson's categories, generated in its own way large amounts of emotional energy and filled the void of national consciousness with a sense of its own exalted vocation. Just as there had been some deep though subtle relationship between the exponent of the imperial self and Jackson's America emerging into self-possession, no less intrinsic a bond existed now between the glorifier of the Anglo-Saxon race and the young giant nation marching to victory over itself and on to world supremacy. The very possibility of this comparison, involving as it does opposite phases in Emerson's career, is as good a proof as any that the imperial self died hard in him.

The time has come to conclude. I hope to have shown how stimulating and provocative I found Professor Anderson's book.

[20] *Journals and Notebooks*, IX, 74.

His notion of the imperial self, even restricted to one author, is comprehensive enough to invite a thorough reexamination of Emerson's value to us, yet sophisticated enough to avoid the pitfalls of emotionalism and historicism. The preacher that he tries to resuscitate for us is at once the product of his time and a very special teacher, less moral than inspired, less inspired than visionary. His problem, with which Professor Anderson deals by flashes of insight rather than by continuous argument, is how to communicate what may very well perish in the naming. Rarely if ever had Emerson's pedagogical embroilment been so deftly conveyed.

To the extent that it is good, or very good, Professor Anderson's book raises expectations that it does not quite gratify. It does not say nearly enough about the linguistic process by which the imperial self fulfils its paradoxical mission of refraining from specific expression while intimating its meaning with sufficient precision. The remarks about abstraction go some distance towards solving the riddle, but they need to be amplified.

My only serious reservation, however, concerns what I would call Professor Anderson's atomization of Emerson. His dismissal of all the writings not belonging to the select canon that he tacitly builds up results in a dwindling of the writer and the cultural figure. There is about Emerson's achievement a totality and a consistency which are admirable and at the same time a little frightening. In his preface, Professor Anderson takes gently to task the critics of earlier generations for unwittingly accepting the role of emotional collaborators. His fault, as I see it, is to have been too generous and committed a collaborator of the imperious self in Emerson. He even preferred to return a verdict of death to avoid the embarrassment of having ultimately to confront an imperious American.

Harold Bloom

THE FRESHNESS OF TRANSFORMATION:

EMERSON'S DIALECTICS OF INFLUENCE

WALLACE STEVENS, closing the second part, *It Must Change*, of *Notes toward a Supreme Fiction*, proclaimed the "will to change, a necessitous/ And present way, a presentation," that brings about "the freshness of transformation." But though this transformation "is ourselves," the Seer of Hartford was too wily not to add a customary qualification:

> And that necessity and that presentation
>
> Are rubbings of a glass in which we peer.
> Of these beginnings, gay and green, propose
> The suitable amours. Time will write them down.

Stevens died in 1955, and many suitable amours concerning various beginnings have been proposed since then. Pound, Eliot, Williams, Moore are gone, among other major figures; and Crane and Roethke were ended prematurely in a subsequent generation. Jarrell and Berryman, whose achievements were more equivocal, have taken on some of the curious lustre that attends the circumstances of such deaths. Contemporary American poetry is a more than usually elaborate panorama, replete with schools and programmes, with followers enough for all,

and readers available for only a few. Even the best of our contemporary poets, whether of any grouping or of none, suffer a
burden wholly appropriate to the valley of vision they hope to
have chosen, a burden more important finally than the immediate sorrows of poetic over-population and the erosion of a liter-
ate audience. Peering into the glass of vision, contemporary
poets confront their too-recent giant precursors staring back at
them, inducing a profound anxiety that hides itself, but cannot
be evaded totally. The partial evasions of this anxiety can be
identified simply as the styles and strategies of contemporary
verse, despite the overt manifestos to the contrary at which current poets seem more than usually adept. The anxiety of influence, a melancholy at a failure in imaginative priority, still rages
like the dog-star in recent poetry, with the results that Pope observed. Poetically, call ours the Age of Sirius, the actual cultural
equivalent of the fictive counter-cultural Age of Aquarius:

> The dog-star rages! nay 'tis past a doubt,
> All Bedlam, or Parnassus, is let out:
> Fire in each eye, and papers in each hand,
> They rave, recite, and madden round the land.

I write these pages after passing an educational hour watching
an array of revolutionary bards, black and white, chanting on
television. Their exhilarating apparent freedom from the anxiety
of influence does not render even the most inchoate rhapsodes
free of so necessitous a malady. Mixed into the tide of rhetoric
came the recognizable detritus of the precursors, ranging from
the American Sublime of Whitman to the sublime bathos of the
Imamu Baraka, yet containing some surprises—of Edna Millay
shining clear in a black poetess, or of Edgar Guest in a revolutionary balladeer, or of Ogden Nash in a particularly ebullient
open-former.

   If we move to the other extreme of contemporary achievement, say Ashbery's *Fragment* or Ammons' *Saliences*, then we confront, as readers, far more intense cases of the anxiety of influence, for Ashbery and Ammons, and a few others in their generation, have matured into strong poets. Their best work, like Robert Penn Warren's or Roethke's or Elizabeth Bishop's, begins to demand the same immense effort of the whole being to absorb and resist as is required by the strongest American poets born in the last three decades of the nineteenth century: Robinson, Frost, Stevens, Pound, Moore, Williams, Eliot, Aiken, Ransom, Jeffers, Cummings, Crane. Perhaps no single reader greatly admires all of these dozen—I do not—though the work seems to abide, admired or not. Pound and Williams primarily, Stevens more recently, Frost and Eliot now rather less so, have been the principal influences upon American poets born in the twentieth century, yet all of these twelve poets have descendants, and all of them induce massive anxieties of influence, though the Pound-Williams schools (there are clearly several) emulate their precursors by a remarkable (and damaging) overt refusal to recognize such anxieties. But poets, for three hundred years now, at least, have joined in denying these anxieties even as they more and more strongly manifest them in their poems.

The war of American poets against influence is part of our Emersonian heritage, manifested first in the great triad of "The Divinity School Address," "The American Scholar," and "Self-Reliance." This heritage can be traced in Thoreau, Whitman, Dickinson, and quite directly again in Robinson and Frost, in the architectural writings of Sullivan and Wright, in the *Essays Before a Sonata* of Charles Ives. The less direct heritage is more relevant to any brooding on the negative aspects of poetic influence, centering partly on Pound and Williams (where it is refracted through Whitman) and partly on Stevens, who disliked the very idea of influence.

This distaste is a proper characteristic of all Modern (mean-

ing post-Enlightenment or Romantic) poets, but peculiarly so of
American poets coming after our prophet (however now unhon-
ored) Emerson. I like Charles Ives' remark upon Emerson's am-
bitions: "His essay on the pre-soul (which he did not write)
treats of that part of the over-soul's influence on unborn ages,
and attempts the impossible only when it stops attempting it."
Call Emerson the over-soul, and then contemplate his influence
upon American poets who had read him (like Jeffers) and those
who had not, but who read him in his poetic descendants (like
Crane, who read his Emerson in Whitman). It can be called the
only poetic influence that counsels against itself, and against the
idea of influence. Perhaps in consequence, it has been the most
pervasive of American poetic influences, though partly unrecog-
nized. In nineteenth-century America, it operated as much by
negation (Poe, Melville, Hawthorne), as by discipleship
(Thoreau, Very, Whitman) or by a dialectical blend of the two
relations (Dickinson, Tuckerman, the Jameses).

In a Journal entry (21 July 1837) Emerson recorded an insight that made possible his three anti-influence oration-essays of
1837–1840:

> Courage consists in the conviction that they with whom
> you contend are no more than you. If we believed in the ex-
> istence of strict *individuals*, natures, that is, not radically
> identical but unknown[,] immeasurable, we should never
> dare to fight.[1]

This striking use of "individuals" manifests Emerson's acute
apprehension of the sorrows of poetic influence, even as he de-
clines to share these sorrows. If the new poet succumbs to a
vision of the precursor as the Sublime, "unknown, immeasur-

[1] Emerson, *Journals and Miscellaneous Notebooks*, ed. W. H. Gilman
and others (Cambridge, Mass., 1960–   ), V, 344–45.

able," then the great contention with the dead father will be lost. We can remember such ambivalent titans of intra-textuality as the quasi-nature deity, Wordsworth, of the later nineteenth century, and in our time that Gnostic divinity, Yeats, and our own current daemon of the American Sublime, Stevens. Emerson, shrewdest of all visionaries, early perceived the accurate enemy in the path of aspiring youth: "Genius is always sufficiently the enemy of genius by over-influence."

Though we rightly blame Emerson for our capitalistic reactionaries as well as for our shamanistic revolutionaries, for the whole range that goes from Henry Ford to the Whole Earth Catalog, his own meditations forestall our observations. His broodings against influence, starting in 1837, took their origins in the great business Depression of that year. Confronting individualism in its terrible freedom, Emerson developed a characteristic antithetical notion of the individual: "Every man is an infinitely repellent orb, and holds his individual being on that condition." Most remarkably, the journal-meditations move to a great self-recognition on May 26, 1837:

> Who shall define to me an Individual? I behold with awe & delight many illustrations of the One Universal Mind. I see my being imbedded in it. As a plant in the earth so I grow in God. I am only a form of him. He is the soul of Me. I can even with a mountainous aspiring say, *I am God*, by transferring my *Me* out of the flimsy & unclean precinct of my body, my fortunes, my private will.... Yet why not always so? How came the Individual thus armed and impassioned to parricide thus murderously inclined ever to traverse & kill the divine life? Ah wicked Manichee! Into that dim problem I cannot enter. A believer in Unity, a seer of Unity, I yet behold two....[2]

[2] *Journals and Notebooks*, V, 336–37.

The enormous split here is central in Emerson, pervades his conflicting ideas of influence, and is as relevant to contemporary poets as it was to Whitman, Robinson, Stevens, Crane, Roethke. Turning off the television set, I open the Sunday book supplement of the newspaper to behold a letter from Joyce Carol Oates, novelist, poet, critic, that replies to a reviewer:

> It is a fallacy of our time, hopefully coming to an end, that "individuals" are competitive and what one does lessens possibilities for another.... I believe that some day...all this wasteful worrying about who owns what, who "owns" a portion of art, will be finished.... In America, we need to get back to Whitman as our spiritual father, to write novels of the kind that might have grown out of "Leaves of Grass." Whitman understood that human beings are not really in competition, excluded from one another. He knew that the role of the poet is to "transfigure" and "clarify"—and, in that way, sanctify....

This moving passage, by an ambitious ephebe of Dreiser, indeed is in Whitman's tradition, and so also in Emerson's. The over-idealization of literature here is normal and necessary for *the writer in a writer*, a self constrained to deny its own selfhood. So Blake grandly noted, after reading Wordsworth, that: "This is all in the highest degree Imaginative and equal to any Poet but not Superior. I cannot think that Real Poets have any competition. None are greatest in the Kingdom of Heaven it is so in Poetry." Critics, who are people in search of images for *acts of reading*, and not of writing, have a different burden, and ought to cease emulating poets in the over-idealization of poetry.

Blake would have insisted that only the Spectre of Urthona, and not the Real Man the Imagination in him, experienced anxiety in reading Wordsworth, or in reading their common father, Milton. Blakean critics, like Frye, too easily join Blake in this insistence. Is this the critic's proper work, to take up the poet's stance? Perhaps there *is* a power or faculty of the Imagination, and certainly all poets *must* go on believing in its existence, yet a critic makes a better start by agreeing with Hobbes that imagination is "decaying sense" and that poetry is written by the same natural man or woman who suffers daily all the inescapable anxieties of competition. This is to say that the imagination refers not to a world of things, but rather that the consciousness of a competing poet is itself a text.

Emerson set out to excel "in Divinity," by which he meant, from the start, "eloquence," to the lasting scandal of certain American moralists from Andrews Norton to Yvor Winters, for Emerson was very much in the Oral Tradition, unlike his nearest contemporary equivalent, Nietzsche. Emerson tells his notebook, on April 18, 1824, a month before his twenty-first birthday: "I cannot dissemble that my abilities are below my ambition. . . ." But he cheerfully adds: "What we ardently love we learn to imitate and so he hopes "to put on eloquence as a robe." [3] Certainly he did, and he learned therefore the first meaning of his idea of Self-Reliance: "Every man has his own voice, manner, eloquence. . . ." He goes on to speak of each person's "sort of love and grief and imagination and action," but these are afterthoughts. The American orator-poet requires singularity in "voice, manner, eloquence," and if he has that, he trusts he has all, or almost all.

The primary Emerson is this confident orator, who as late as 1839 can still say, in his journals, that: "It is the necessity of my nature to shed all influences." Mixed into this primary strain is a yearning *to be influenced*, but only by a Central Man who is yet to come. In 1845, a year before his Bacchic intensity-of-reac-

[3] *Journals and Notebooks*, II, 238, 242.

tion against the Mexican War, Emerson characteristically began those expectations of a new man-god that emerged more fully in 1846. In the 1845 Journals, the tone might be called the apocalyptic wistful:

> We are candidates, we know we are, for influences more subtle and more high than those of talent and ambition. We want a leader, we want a friend whom we have not seen. In the company and fired by the example of a god, these faculties that dream and toss in their sleep would wake. Where is the Genius that shall marshal us the way that we were going? There is a vast residue, an open account ever.
>
> The great inspire us: how they beckon, how they animate, and show their legitimate power in nothing more than their power to misguide us. For the perverted great derange and deject us, and perplex ages with their fame. . . . This is that which the strong genius works upon; the region of destiny, of aspiration, of the unknown. . . .

We might follow Nietzsche, Emerson's admirer, and note that as Apollo apparently represents each new poet's individuation, so Dionysus ought to be emblematic of each poet's return to his subsuming precursors. Some such realization informed Emerson's dilemma, for he believed that poetry came only from Dionysian influx, yet he preached an Apollonian Self-Reliance while fearing the very individuation it would bring. "If only he *sees*, the world will be visible enough," is one Emersonian formula carrying this individuation to the borders of a sublime solipsism. Here, expounding nature's supposed method, is a greater formula:

> His health and greatness consist in his being the channel through which heaven flows to earth, in short, in the fulness in which an ecstatical state takes place in him. It is pitiful to be an artist, when by forbearing to be artists we

> might be vessels filled with the divine overflowings, enriched by the circulations of omniscience and omnipresence. Are there not moments in the history of heaven when the human race was not counted by individuals, but was only the Influenced, was God in distribution, God rushing into multiform benefit? It is sublime to receive, sublime to love, but this lust of imparting as from *us*, this desire to be loved, the wish to be recognized as individuals,—is finite, comes of a lower strain.

Emerson's beautiful confusion *is* beautiful because the conflict is emotional, between equal impulses, and because it cannot be resolved. Influx would make us Bacchic, but *not* individuated poets; Self-Reliance will help make us poets, but "of a lower strain," short of ecstatic possession. Emerson's relative failure as a writer of verse ("failure" only when measured against his enormous basic aspirations) is caused by this conflict, and so is his overvaluation of poetry, *a poetry never yet written*, as he too frequently complains. He asks for a stance simultaneously Dionysiac and Self-reliant, and he does not know how this is to be attained, nor do we. I suggest that the deeper cause for his impossible demand is his inner division on the burden of influx, at once altogether to be desired and yet altogether to be resisted, if it comes to us (as it must) from a precursor no more ultimately Central than ourselves, no less a text than we are.

But this is not just the native strain in Emerson; it is the American burden. It came to him because, at the right time in our cultural history, he bravely opened himself to it, but by opening to it with so astonishing a receptivity to oppositions, he opened all subsequent American artists to the same irreconcilable acceptance of negations. Post-Emersonian American poetry, when compared to post-Wordsworthian British poetry, or post-Goethean German poetry, or French poetry after Hugo, is uniquely open to influencings, and uniquely resistant to all *ideas-of-influence*. From Whitman to our contemporaries, American poets eagerly proclaim that they reject nothing that is best in past poetry, and as desperately succumb to poetic defence mechanisms, or self-malformings, rhetorical tropes run wild, against a crippling anxiety of influence. Emerson, source of our sorrow, remains to be quarried, not so much for a remedy, but for a fuller appreciation of the malady. The crux of the matter is a fundamental question for American poets. It could be phrased: In becoming a poet, is one joining oneself to a company of others or truly becoming a solitary and single one? In a sense, this is the anxiety of *whether* one ever really *became* a poet, a double-anxiety: Did one truly join that company? Did one become truly oneself?

In his essay *Character*, Emerson emphasized the fear of influence:

> Higher natures overpower lower ones by affecting them with a certain sleep. The faculties are locked up, and offer no resistance. Perhaps that is the universal law. When the high cannot bring up the low to itself, it benumbs it, as man charms down the resistance of the lower animals. Men exert on each other a similar occult power. How often has the influence of a true master realized all the tales of magic! A river of command seemed to run down from his eyes into all those who beheld him, a torrent of strong sad light, like an Ohio or Danube, which pervaded them with his thoughts and colored all events with the hue of his mind.[4]

This flood of light, which Emerson taught his descendants to fear, rather curiously ran down upon them from *his* eyes. As he himself said, in the essay *Politics:* "The boundaries of personal

[4] Emerson, *Works*, ed. E. W. Emerson (Boston, 1903–1904), III, 94.

influence it is impossible to fix, as persons are organs of moral or supernatural force." [5] Property, he cunningly added, had the same power. As eloquence, to Emerson, was identical with personal energy, eloquence was necessarily personal property, and the dialectics of energy became the dialectics also of commerce. One can say that for Emerson the imagination *was* linguistic energy.

At his most apocalyptic, as throughout the troubling year 1846, when he wrote his best poems, Emerson again denied the anxiety of influence, as here in "Uses of Great Men" from *Representative Men:*

> We need not fear excessive influence. A more generous trust is permitted. Serve the great. Stick at no humiliation. Grudge no office thou canst render. Be the limb of their body, the breath of their mouth. Compromise thy egotism. Who cares for that, so thou gain aught wider and nobler? Never mind the taunt of Boswellism: the devotion may easily be greater than the wretched pride which is guarding its own skirts. Be another: not thyself, but a Platonist; not a soul, but a Christian; not a naturalist, but a Cartesian; not a poet, but a Shakespearian. In vain, the wheels of tendency will not stop, nor will all the forces of inertia, fear, or of love itself hold thee there. On, and forever onward! [6]

Though this over-protests, it remains haunted by the unfulfillable maxim: "Never imitate." Has Emerson forgotten his own insight, that one must be an inventor to read well? Whatever "we" means, in his passage, it cannot mean what it meant in a great notebook passage behind *Self-Reliance:* "We are a vision." Rather than multiply bewildering instances, of Emerson on all sides of this dark and central idea, we do him most justice by seeking his ultimate balance where always that must be sought, in his

[5] *Works*, III, 205.   [6] *Works*, IV, 29–30.

grandest essay, *Experience*. Solve this, and you have Emerson-on-influence, if he can be solved at all:

> Thus inevitably does the universe wear our color, and every object fall successively into the subject itself. The subject exists, the subject enlarges; all things sooner or later fall into place. As I am, so I see; use what language we will, we can never say anything but what we are; Hermes, Cadmus, Columbus, Newton, Bonaparte are the mind's ministers. Instead of feeling a poverty when we encounter a great man, let us treat the newcomer like a travelling geologist who passes through our estate and shows us good slate, or limestone, or anthracite, in our brush pasture. The partial action of each strong mind in one direction is a telescope for the objects on which it is pointed. But every other part of knowledge is to be pushed to the same extravagance, ere the soul attains her due sphericity.[7]

The blindness of the strong, Emerson implies, necessarily constitutes insight. Is the insight of the strong also blindness? Can a soul duly spherical be enough of an *unseeing* soul to go on writing poetry? Here is the gnomic poem that introduces *Experience:*

> The lords of life, the lords of life,—
> I saw them pass,
> In their own guise,
> Like and unlike,
> Portly and grim,
> Use and Surprise,
> Surface and Dream,
> Succession swift, and spectral Wrong,
> Temperament without a tongue,
> And the inventor of the game
> Omnipresent without name;—

[7] *Works*, III, 79–80.

Some to see, some to be guessed,
They marched from east to west:
Little man, least of all,
Among the legs of his guardians tall,
Walked about with puzzled look.
Him by the hand dear Nature took,
Dearest Nature, strong and kind,
Whispered, Darling, never mind!
To-morrow they will wear another face,
The founder thou! these are thy race! [8]

This is the Emerson of about 1842, and if no longer a Primary, he is not quite a Secondary Man. The lords of life (and *Life* was the first title for *Experience*) are a rather dubious sevenfold to inspire any poet, and the more-than-Wordsworthian homely nurse, Nature, offers little comfort. If these are the gods, then man is sensible to be puzzled. But it all goes with a diabolically cheerful (though customarily awkward) lilt, and the indubitable prophet of our literary self-reliance seems as outrageously cheerful as ever. There aren't any good models in this procession, and man, Nature assures us, is *their* model, but we are urged to yet another mode of Self-Reliance anyway. "Ne te quaesiveris extra" (Do not seek yourself outside yourself), but what is it to seek yourself even within yourself? Does the essay *Experience*, in giving us, as I think it does, a vision beyond skepticism, give us also any way out of the double-bind of poetic influence?

"We thrive by casualties," Emerson says, and while he means "random occurrences" he could as well have meant "losses." But these would have been casual losses, given up to "those who are powerful obliquely and not by the direct stroke." Very charmingly Emerson says of these masters that "one gets the cheer of their light without paying too great a tax." Such an

[8] *Works*, III, 43.

influence Emerson himself hoped to be, but Thoreau and even Whitman paid a heavy tax for Emersonian light, and I suspect many contemporary Americans still pay something, whether or not they have read Emerson, since his peculiar relevance now is that we seem to read him merely by living here, in this place still somehow his, and not our own. His power over us attains an elevation in an astonishing recovery from skepticism that suddenly illuminates *Experience:*

> And we cannot say too little of our constitutional necessity of seeing things under private aspects. . . . And yet is the God the native of these bleak rocks. . . . We must hold hard to this poverty, however scandalous, and by more vigorous self-recoveries, after the sallies of action, possess our axis more firmly.[9]

After this, Emerson is able to give us a blithe prose-list of "the lords of life": "Illusion, Temperament, Succession, Surface, Surprise, Reality, Subjectiveness," and in accepting these he gives us also his escape from conflicting attitudes towards influence: "All I know is reception; I am and I have: but I do not get, and when I have fancied I had gotten anything, I found I did not." But there speaks the spheral man, the all-but-perfect solipsist who made Thoreau almost despair, and whom Whitman emulated only to end as a true poet in the grief-ridden palinode of "As I Ebbed With the Ocean of Life." Charles Ives, deeply under the influence of Emerson's late *Prudence,* movingly remarks: "Everyone should have the opportunity of not being over-influenced." Stevens, a less candid Emersonian, is far closer to *Experience* in his ecstatic momentary victories over influence:

[9] *Works,* III, 81.

I have not but I am and as I am, I am.
. . . .
. . . Perhaps,
The man-hero is not the exceptional monster,
But he that of repetition is most master.

Emerson says: "I am and I have," and, because he receives
without self-appropriation, "I do not get." Stevens says: "I have
not but I am," because he does not receive, but appropriates for
himself through mastering the repetition of his own never-end-
ing meditation upon self. Emerson is the more perfect solipsist,
and yet also the more generous spirit, thus getting the better of
it both ways. Stevens, the better poet but the much less transcendent consciousness, is less persuasive in proclaiming an ultimate Self-Reliance. In this, he does not differ however from all
our Emersonian poets, whether voluntary like Whitman, Robinson, Frost or involuntary like Dickinson and Melville. Stevens
too, who saw himself as "A new scholar replacing an older one,"
became another involuntary ephebe of the Supreme Fiction of
our literature, Emersonian individualism, which remains our
most troublesome trope.

Recoiling from the consequences of an all-repellent individualism, Emerson opted first for Dionysian influx, and later for
the dominance of that other Orphic presence, Ananke, who opposed herself to the individual as his own limitations perceived
under the mark of a different aesthetic, the beauty of Fate. For
Emerson's was an aesthetic of *use*, a properly pragmatic American aesthetic, that came to fear imaginative entropy as the worst
foe of the adverting or questing mind, seeking to make of its
own utility of eloquence a vision of universal good.

What can be used can be used up; this is what Geoffrey
Hartman calls "the anxiety of demand," a version of which is

enacted in a fundamental Romantic genre, the crisis-lyric. Does the achieved poem give confidence that the next poem can be written? An Idealizing critic, even one of great accomplishment, evidently can believe that poets are concerned, as poets, only with the anxiety of form, and not at all with the anxieties of influence and of demand; but all form, however personalized, stems from influx, and all form, however depersonalized, shapes itself against depletion, and so seeks to meet demand. Beneath the anxiety of demand is a ghost of all precursor-obsessions: the concern that inspiration may fail, whereas the strong illusion persists that inspiration could not fail the precursor, for did he not inspire the still-struggling poet?

Emerson's inspiration never failed, in part because it never wholly came to him, or if it did then it came mixed with considerable prudence, and generally arrived in the eloquence of prose. If the anxiety-of-influence descends as a myth of the father, then we can venture that the anxiety-of-demand is likely to manifest itself through imagistic concealments of the mother or Muse. In Stevens, particularly in the late phase of *The Auroras of Autumn* and *The Rock*, the concealment is withdrawn:

> Farewell to an idea. . . . The mother's face,
> The purpose of the poem, fills the room . . .

But Stevens, for all his late bleakness, was preternaturally fecund, and did not suffer greatly from the anxiety-of-demand, nor did Emerson. Whitman did, and that sorrow still requires exploration by his readers. The anxiety induced by a vision of the imaginative father, however, is strongly Stevens', as here in the *Auroras:*

> The father sits
> In space, wherever he sits, of bleak regard.
> As one that is strong in the bushes of his eyes.

He says no to no and yes to yes. He says yes
To no; and in saying yes he says farewell.

This Jehovah-like affirmer, whose eyes have replaced the burning bush, is a composite figure, with Emerson and Whitman important components, since of all Stevens' precursors they most extravagantly said yes. The saying of farewell is equivocal. Stevens, more forcibly than Pound, exemplifies making it new through the freshness of transformation, and more comprehensively than Williams persuades us that the difficulties of cultural heritage cannot be overcome through evasions. Emerson, ancestor to all three, would have found in Stevens what he once had found in Whitman, a rightful heir of the American quest for a Self-Reliance founded upon a complete self-knowledge.

Contemporary American poetry, written in the large shadowings of Pound, Williams, Stevens, and their immediate progeny, is an impossibly heroic quest wholly in the Emersonian tradition, another variation on the native strain. The best of our contemporary poets show an astonishing energy of response to the sorrow of influence that forms so much of the hidden subject of their work. As heirs, sometimes unknowing, of Emerson, they receive also his heartening faith that: "Eloquence is the appropriate organ of the highest personal energy," and so they can participate also in the noblest of Emersonian conscious indulgences in the Optative Mood, the belief that influence, for a potentially strong poet, is only energy that comes from a precursor, as Emerson says, "of the same turn of mind as his own, and who sees much farther on his own way than he." On this Emersonian implicit theory of the imagination, literary energy is drawn from language and not from nature, and the influence-relationship takes place between words *and* words, and not between subjects. I am a little unhappy to find Emerson, even in one of his aspects, joining Nietzsche as a precursor of Jacques Derrida and Paul de Man, twin titans of deconstruction, and so I want to conclude by juxtaposing Derrida with Emerson on the anxiety of influence. First, Derrida:

> The concept of centered structure is in fact the concept of a freeplay based on a fundamental ground, a freeplay which is constituted upon a fundamental immobility and a reassuring certitude, which is itself beyond the reach of the freeplay. With this certitude anxiety can be mastered, for anxiety is invariably the result of a certain mode of being implicated in the game, of being caught by the game, of being as it were from the very beginning at stake in the game.

Against this, Emerson, from the essay *Nominalist and Realist*:

> For though gamesters say that the cards beat all the players, though they were never so skilful, yet in the contest we are now considering, the players are also the game, and share the power of the cards.

Nietzsche, according to Derrida, inaugurated the decentering that Freud, Heidegger, Lévi-Strauss and, most subversively, Derrida himself have accomplished in the Beulah-lands of Interpretation. Though I am myself an uneasy quester after lost meanings, I still conclude I favor a kind of interpretation that seeks to restore and redress meaning, rather than primarily deconstruct meaning. To de-idealize our vision of texts is a good, but a limited good, and I follow Emerson, as against Nietzsche, in declining to make of de-mystification the principal end of dialectical thought in criticism.

Marcuse, introducing Hegel yet sounding like a Kabbalist, insists that dialectical thinking must make the absent present "because the greater part of the truth is in that which is absent."

Speech and "positive" thinking are false because they are "part of a mutilated whole." A Marxist dialectician like Adorno shows us clearly what dialectical thinking is in our time; the thinker self-consciously thinks about his thinking in the very act of intending the objects of his thought. Emerson, in *Nominalist and Realist*, still a genuinely startling text, simply says that: "No sentence will hold the whole truth, and the only way in which we can be just, is by giving ourselves the lie. . . ." That is a wilder variety of dialectical thinking than most Post-Hegelian Europeans attempt, and Emerson is in consequence as maddening as he is ingratiating. For, in Emerson, dialectical thought does not fulfill the primary function of fighting off the idealistic drive of an expanding consciousness. Both in his Transcendental and in his Necessitarian phases, Emerson does not worry about ending in solipsism; he is only too happy to reach the transparency of solipsism whenever he can. He is very much Wittgenstein's Schopenhauerian solipsist who knows he is right in what he *means*, and who knows also that he is in error in what he *says*. The solipsism of Emerson's Transcendentalism issues finally in the supra-realism of the Necessitarianism of his last great book, the magnificent *The Conduct of Life*. Dialectical thinking in Emerson does not attempt to bring us back to the world of things and of other selves, but only to a world of language, and so its purpose is never to *negate* what is directly before us. From a European perspective, probably, Emersonian thinking is not so much dialectical as it is plain crazy, and I suspect that even Blake would have judged Emerson to be asserting that: "Without negations there is no progression," a negation being for Blake opposed to a genuinely dialectical contrary. Yet Nietzsche, who could tolerate so few of his own contemporaries, delighted in Emerson, and seems to have understood Emerson very well. And I think Nietzsche particularly understood that Emerson had come to prophesy not a de-centering, as Nietzsche had, and as Derrida and de Man are brilliantly accomplishing, but a peculiarly American *re-centering*, and with it an American mode of interpretation, one that we have begun (but only begun) to develop, from Whitman and Peirce down to Stevens and Kenneth Burke, a mode that *is* intra-textual, but that stubbornly remains logocentric, and that still follows Emerson in valorizing eloquence, the inspired voice, *over* the scene of writing. Emerson, who said he unsettled all questions, first put literature into question for us and now survives to question our questioners.

Albert Gelpi

EMERSON: THE PARADOX OF ORGANIC FORM

ALTHOUGH EMERSON PUBLISHED only two volumes of verse, he insisted that in all his thinking and writing he was a poet; such was his encompassing activity and purpose in prose and verse. But while Emerson's prose has received extended critical attention, his verse needs and deserves more study than it has received so far, and needs more perceptive study than the assumptions of the New Criticism and other schools of normative and formalist criticism have allowed in the academy until quite recently. The reason is simple: formalist criticism makes assumptions—about the sources of poetry, the relation of the poem to experience, the function of language and form, in short about the entire activity of the poet—which run counter to all of Emerson's assumptions. By formalist norms Emerson's poems seem flawed by loose ends, careless structure and slack diction, but those norms are largely irrelevant to what Emerson is doing, or at any rate attempting. We now see more clearly that we must develop a criticism whose axioms and procedures are consonant with Emerson's poetry (and that of the American poets who follow in his wake); in fact, we need a criticism which springs from those poems and so can open them up for us and allow us to enter them and participate in them on their own terms.

This essay, therefore, is not about Emerson's poems but

about the underlying principles of his poetics, so that we can begin to attune ourselves more acutely to the poems than the training of most of us would permit. It is important to understand Emerson's poetics, with all its ambivalences and paradoxes, not just for what it accomplished in Emerson's work but also for what it engendered in the dynamics of language and form in the American tradition thereafter. Emerson's theory itself is part of the Romantic rejection of neoclassical formalism, but its radical and revolutionary character stems from the fact that Emerson brought to certain Romantic notions a Yankee earnestness and literalness that carried them much further in theory and practice than English and continental Romantics had dared. His notion of the aim and activity of the poet so splendidly epitomized the idealistic strain in the New England (and American) character that his words blazed a path for others to explore, extend, and depart from on their own excursions, and that path is the main line of the American tradition.

At the beginning of *Nature* a simple statement carries momentous psychological, moral, and aesthetic implications: the poet is "he whose eye can integrate all the parts." The poet as "eye" is far more than a naturalist observing phenomena in minute detail like Frederick Goddard Tuckerman out in Greenfield or even Emerson's friend Thoreau camping out on Emerson's ground at Walden Pond. For all of Emerson's love of the woods and lakes around Concord, Emerson would write an essay on the "Natural History of Intellect" while Thoreau was to write the "Natural History of Massachusetts." Emerson would continue to complain that naturalists, with their labels and discriminations, were always pointing to the particular instead of the universal: "Our botany is all names, not powers. . . ." In old age Emerson cited Blake's goal of seeing through the eye, not with it, but already in *Nature* in 1836 he had recognized that "the eye is the best of artists" because it reveals to the imagination—not just to the intellective understanding—"the integrity of impression made by manifold natural objects." [1] There are two kinds of seeing: with the eye and through the eye, sensory and spiritual; the second proceeds from the first but cannot be accounted for or bound by mere visual impressions:

> To speak truly, few adult persons can see nature. Most persons do not see the sun. At least they have a very superficial seeing. The sun illuminates only the eye of the man, but shines into the eye and heart of the child. The lover of nature is he whose inward and outward senses are still truly adjusted to each other. . . .[2]

The eye is not just the ocular sense; the "eye" orders all the senses and faculties in a single experiential perception of the interpenetration of all things. Again and again the essays specify the eye as the poetic organ: the "cultivated eye"; "the wise eye"; "the world's eye"; "the comprehensive eye"; "the plastic power of the human eye"; "the supernatural eye."

The miracle of incarnation transpires not just in church sacraments but in all life, which is sacramental; Emerson used a theological term to make his point: "this contemporary insight is transubstantiation, the conversion of daily bread into the holiest symbols. . . ." [3] In *Nature* Emerson tried to describe this conversion. It is a famous and familiar passage, but it deserves quo-

---

[1] *Nature*, in *Nature, Addresses & Lectures, The Complete Works of Ralph Waldo Emerson*, ed. Edward Waldo Emerson, Centenary Edition (Boston, 1903–1904), I, 8, 15; "Beauty," *The Conduct of Life, Works*, VI, 281. In these notes references to Emerson will cite this edition, abbreviated as *Works*; and the volume *Nature, Addresses & Lectures* will henceforth be abbreviated as *NAL*.

[2] *Nature, NAL, Works*, I, 8–9.

[3] "Poetry and Imagination," *Letters & Social Aims, Works*, VIII, 35.

tation here because, like the fifth section of Whitman's "Song of Myself," it presents the generative experience from which the whole work and the whole vision proceed. The statements are at once declarative and open-ended; they set down an experience of vision beyond analysis.

> In the woods, too, a man casts off his years, as the snake his slough, and at what period soever of life, is always a child. . . . There I feel that nothing can befall me in life,—no disgrace, no calamity (leaving me my eyes), which nature cannot repair. Standing on the bare ground,—my head bathed by the blithe air, and uplifted into infinite space,— all mean egotism vanishes. I become a transparent eye-ball; I am nothing; I see all; the currents of the Universal Being circulate through me; I am part or parcel of God.[4]

The punning identity of the pronoun "I" and the "eye" as its central and coordinating organ punctuates the stages of the process: I expand into the cosmos until my immensity coincides with cosmic Unity. The imaginative process, then, is a penetration into the divine mystery of life and living, an inseeing and not just a seeing; and this insight operates simultaneously as expansion and integration.

In *Representative Men* Emerson said: "Two cardinal facts lie forever at the base; the one and the two.—1. Unity, or Identity; and 2. Variety . . . Oneness and Otherness. It is impossible to speak or think without embracing both." The perception of Variety and Unity is the function respectively of the different cognitive faculties of Understanding and Reason. Understanding is the logical-rational faculty which operates deductively and inductively on the data supplied by the senses; Reason is the transcendental faculty which sees intuitively universal truths in Na-

[4] *Nature, NAL, Works,* I, 9–10.

ture. This distinction became standard as the German transcendentalist philosophers came into England and America through people like Coleridge and Carlyle. [In the "Discipline" chapter of *Nature* Emerson stated it in these words: "The understanding adds, divides, combines, measures, and finds nutriment and room for its activity in this worthy scene. Meantime, Reason transfers all these lessons into its own world of thought, by perceiving the analogy that marries Matter and Mind" (p. 36). Experience, therefore, brings the mind to unriddle itself and embrace the two in the one; the data which the Understanding gathers concerning natural and psychological phenomena constellate in the Unity which Transcendental Reason intuits. For Emerson, Understanding and Reason are only the philosophical terms for the poet's seeing with the eye and seeing through the eye. The very recognition that "the world I converse with in the city and in the farms, is not the world I *think*," begins the process of reintegration, and further acts of perception begin to bind the perceiver to the perceived both naturally and transcendentally, concentric with "the eye of Reason." The Imagination is a function of Reason.[5]

Thus in the essay on "The Poet," Emerson summed up the power of insight and extended it into the more problematical area of articulation and expression:

> The poet is the person in whom those powers are in balance, the man without impediment, who sees and handles that which others dream of, traverses the whole scale of experience, and is representative of man, in virtue of being the largest power to receive and to impart.[6]

[5] "Plato; or, the Philosopher," *Representative Men, Works, IV*, 47–48; "Experience," *Essays Second Series, Works*, III, 84; *Nature, NAL, Works*, I 49. Henceforth *Essays Second Series* will be abbreviated as *Essays II*.

[6] "The Poet," *Essays II, Works*, III, 6.

The poet's "power to receive and to impart"—a double power; vision alone is insufficient, even for the seer. "Always the seer is a sayer" as well; his secondary but essential role is "the Namer or Language-maker." The poet must write poems, for "the man is only half himself, the other half is his expression." [7] Even with the insight of Imagination only the poet's doubling back on himself to formulate and issue his own statement can bring experience to fuller consciousness; the wordless Reason incarnates itself in natural forms, in human experience, and so in human speech.

The three axioms posited at the beginning of the "Language" chapter of *Nature* make the same point by moving in the other direction, from words to things to spirit, in a chain of correspondences. Again these familiar sentences are crucial to Emerson's poetic theory:

1. Words are signs of natural facts.
2. Particular natural facts are symbols of particular spiritual facts.
3. Nature is the symbol of spirit.

The tongue moves with the eye and with "the eye of Reason." Emerson's theory of language assumes that words are at root so connected with objects that the primitive meaning of all words, even abstractions, designates an object. He gave examples in the "Language" chapter and returned to the subject often, as here in "The Poet":

> For though the origin of most of our words is forgotten, each word was at first a stroke of genius, and obtained currency because for the moment it symbolized the world to

[7] "The Divinity School Address," *NAL, Works,* I, 134; "The Poet," *Essays II, Works,* III, 21, 37, 5, 7.

the first speaker and to the hearer. . . . Language is fossil
poetry.

The poet's task is to save language from dead forms—fossiliza-
tion and abstraction—by constantly making it new (as Pound's
phrase goes): "Every word was once a poem. Every new relation
is a new word." Or should ideally be. Emerson's linguistic assumptions may be scientifically questionable, but they link his
metaphysics and his aesthetics. The "natural sayer" will in
theory make language correspond immediately to experience by
attaching words as much as possible to the objects they signify.
From the same premises Thoreau says in "Walking": "he would
be a poet . . . who nailed words to their primitive senses, as
farmers drive down stakes in the spring, which the frost has
heaved; who derived his words as often as he used them,—
transplanted them to the page with earth adhering to their
roots. . . ." [8]

So organic is the finding of words that the "natural sayer"
cannot rely primarily on training and discipline and practice to
perfect his technique and sharpen his tools. In fact, he must be
wary of the danger inherent in a mistaken trust in external arrangements. No craftsman applying his developed skills to inchoate materials, Emerson's "Language-maker" would, to the
contrary, be the "receiver," the "instrument," the "bard of the
Holy Ghost" "passive to the superincumbent spirit." In the
open moments between the "incoming" and "receding of God,"
he is "nothing else than a good, free, vascular organization,
whereinto the universal spirit freely flows." The poet is not the
cool catalyst, as T.S. Eliot came to claim in his argument for
impersonality, but the vascular tissue and living membrane;

[8] *Nature, NAL, Works,* I, 25.

Emerson's analogy is not chemistry but biology. After the inspiration the bard's words imitate the workings of Spirit in Nature, or such is that aim:

> For poetry was all written before time was, and whenever we are so finely organized that we can penetrate into that region where the air is music, we hear those primal warblings and attempt to write them down, but we lose ever and anon a word or a verse and substitute something of our own, and thus miswrite the poem. The men of more delicate ear write down these cadences more faithfully, and these transcripts, though imperfect, become the songs of the nations.

On the highest level the poet's ingenuity and technical skill can even be an inhibitive intrusion on the creative process; to the extent that he concentrates on making language he may be interfering with the flow of inspiration to and through the medium.[9] Paradise, Pound would repeat in *The Pisan Cantos* against Baudelaire's aestheticism, is not artificial but is the *tao*, or the divine process of nature.

Consequently Emerson's theory had to be of two minds about the efficacy of language. All words must be nailed to things, and yet "all the facts in Nature are nouns of the intellect, and make the grammar of the eternal language." The poet must speak, but as the essential poetry moves into language, it will be at once exalted as the "word" of God and halting as human speech. To the extent that the poet is the instrument through which Reason expresses itself, language is invaluable; to the ex-

[9] *Nature, NAL, Works,* I, 47; "Beauty," *The Conduct of Life, Works,* VI, 283; "The Divinity School Address," *NAL, Works,* I, 143; "Literary Ethics," *NAL, Works,* I, 165; "The Poet," *Essays II, Works,* III, 8.

tent to which the poet speaks his own associations, language is a
noisy distraction. On the one side lies Silence, on the other gibberish; and in the middle the situation is complicated by the fact
that Silence can only express itself on the poet's tongue and by
the fact that as the poet's tongue strives to express Silence it concentrates its many, noisy words towards a single, indiscrim-
inate, primitive syllable, like the Hindu mystic repeating "Om"
till he returns to unconsciousness or pure consciousness. Is that
"Om" wisdom or gibberish? The mystic says that it conveys All
and Nothing, a false distinction which exists only in human
speech.

But by its very nature language must negotiate that middle
ground without lapsing into All or Nothing, into Silence or gibberish. For, to someone like Emerson, words are (or can be) the
irreplaceable translations from the wordless sublime moving
through time and space: the oracle "has only to open his mouth,
and it [universal nature] speaks." Yet even the oracle's words,
not to mention those of less inspired mortals, will necessarily
convey only a "corrupt version" of his unspeakable meaning.
Lao Tsu begins *Tao Te Ching* with: "The Tao that can be told is
not the eternal Tao. The name that can be named is not the
eternal name." Emerson said that words "cannot cover the dimensions of what is in truth. They break, chop, and impoverish
it." Even words rooted in things are only a gesture toward the
meaning of things. Since the paradox of language is that "words
are finite organs of the infinite mind," even the successful poem
will be an incomplete articulation. Language has form, and so
limits, but meaning does not; or, in the words of a couplet
whose halting inadequacy is most imitative, "The great Idea baf-
fles wit, / Language falters under it." At best, effort and subtle
discriminations and the filing of lines and cadences can clarify a

poem up to a certain point, and at worst they can break the circuit of inspiration. The "true poet" learns to acknowledge humbly that "there is a higher work for Art than the arts." [10]

Emerson's ambivalence about language seemed to lead him into contradiction. If words are literally the organs of the infinite mind, the poet can do no better than merely submit, but if they are his words, the poet is to some extent and at some level responsible for what he says. At times Emerson spoke as though inspiration were a matter of unconscious receptivity, almost of automatic writing. Yeats claimed that *A Vision* derived from his wife's automatic writing and generated images and metaphors for his poems, but he made no claim of automatic writing for himself as composer either of *A Vision* or of his poems. There have been Romantic claims of more or less spontaneous creation—most notably perhaps Coleridge's account of the writing of "Kubla Khan." Even more extremely, closer to home and farther down the line, Jack Kerouac said that he tried to open his mouth and let the Holy Ghost speak, as Jesus had urged His disciples; Ginsberg usually prepares an audience for his incantatory poems by long repetitions of "Om" and other chanted prayers. Can Emerson really believe that a poet is a simple medium? For that matter is it simple to be a medium? Consciousness cannot be excluded by fiat, especially not in the act of writing. The inspiration may be spontaneous and unconscious, but the composition cannot be. As a practicing poet, Emerson knew this. Ginsberg submits to revision the poems which he later

[10] "Beauty," *The Conduct of Life, Works*, VI, 304; "Literary Ethics," *NAL, Works*, I, 165; "The Poet," *Essays II, Works*, III, 24–26; *Nature, NAL, Works*, I, 46–46; *Poems, Works*, IX, 359; "Art," *Essays First Series, Works*, II, 363; Lao Tsu, *Tao Te Ching*, tr. Gia Fu Feng & Jane English (New York, 1972), p. 3. Henceforth *Essays First Series* will be abbreviated as *Essays I*.

reads after those incantations. Even something as close to automatic writing as Kerouac's "spontaneous prose" and verse appears to be is not always unrevised; *On the Road*, his most widely admired book, went through several versions.

Emerson's ambivalence is part of the larger Romantic dilemma. For all his vaunting claims, Shelley too acknowledged, in his *Defence of Poetry*, that the inspired poet comes to words only as the wordless inspiration is fading; the challenge to the Romantic poet is somehow to validate his inspiration. Emerson's essays and poems took a deliberately extreme position in enunciating the notion of a poetry whose source lies outside the poet but whose realization in language and form is through the agency of the poet. Coleridge had also distinguished between poetry and the made poem. The activity begins in the encounter of the poet and nature through an impulse, presumed to come from above, which emerges from the poet's psychic unconscious. He must submit to these energies breaking into consciousness as words and attend that their expression corresponds to the experience. The poem is made from the poetry as nonverbal or preverbal instinctual impulses find articulation, take direction and cohere. "Hence," declared Emerson, "the necessity of speech and song; hence these throbs and heart-beatings in the orator, at the door of the assembly, to the end namely that thought may be ejaculated as Logos, or Word." The paradox for the prophet, whether poet or orator (and the prophetic call links the two) is that, unlike the talkers who speak "*from without,* as spectators merely," he must "speak *from within,* or from experience," making sure that the utterance published under his name coheres to tally the ejaculative, eruptive experience inside.[11]

[11] "The Poet," *Essays II, Works*, III, 40; "The Over-Soul," *Essays I, Works*, II, 287.

Finally, therefore, Emerson's contradictory statements can be seen as related in the attempt to describe the gestation and birth of the poem: a process so subtle that the poet cannot sort out, in the matrix of his psyche where it all grows, unconscious intuition from deliberated choice. Ex post facto theory dissects what is fused in the act. The seeming contradictions are two ways of accounting for organic poetry: the paradox of its inspiration and execution. We think of the poet's Muse: a transpersonal inspiration. But since he encounters the Muse and expresses the Muse only in the forms of Nature and since the poem gestates in his mind, not hers, the process is mutually procreative. Does she shape the poem out of him, or does he shape her in the poem? Both; the father and the mother of the poem are one, the poet is Eros and Psyche.

Emerson felt impelled to take an extreme position in arguing for the mysterious sources and resources of poetry in part because of the literary situation in mid-nineteenth-century America. There were many—and Emerson probably had Edgar Allan Poe and Alfred Tennyson in mind—who called themselves poets but who, he believed, had only technical virtuosity:

> For we do not speak now of men of poetical talents, or of industry and skill in metre, but of the true poet. I took part in a conversation the other day concerning a recent writer of lyrics, a man of subtle mind, whose head appeared to be a music-box of delicate tunes and rhythms, and whose skill and command of language we could not sufficiently praise. But when the question arose whether he was not only a lyrist but a poet, we were obliged to confess that he is plainly a contemporary, not an eternal man.

"The finish of the verses" is a consequence of poetry rather than an originating constituent. Poetry does not arise from or reside in the poem, but vice versa; the experience is not verbal, and language is no substitute for vision. In Emerson's mind Poe's fatal mistake lay in not understanding that "it is not metres but a metre-making argument that makes a poem." The intricacy of Poe's forms and the musicality of his language only confirmed him a victim of his "poetical talents." By contrast Emerson said of Thoreau that "his genius was better than his talent." He lacked "lyric facility and technical skill" and his verses were often unfinished. But even when he wrote inferior poems, "he had the source of poetry" so surely that "he held all actual written poems in very light esteem." The difference, Emerson says elsewhere, is the difference between the poet who speaks from character and the poet who speaks from language. So basic is the distinction between poetry and the poem that for Emerson Poe is a bad poet who often wrote good poems while Thoreau is a good poet who often wrote clumsy poems.[12]

All of this is not to say that Emerson had no regard for poetic form, but rather that he regarded poetic form with the same ambivalence that he felt toward language, and for the same reasons; form, like the words which comprise it, is both the received and the achieved. The poet cannot dictate the form arbitrarily but he has to help it define itself from within. For all his inveighing against artifice, Emerson was by no means oblivious to craft and structure; he was challenging Poe's notion of form with his own. If the poem was to incarnate the experience, then the whole poem would have to imitate the dimensions and shape of reality. Emerson said, after all, that a metre-*making* argument *makes* the poem. If a rigid and preconceived form—*forma ab extra*, Coleridge had called it—distorts words to its own shape, then organic form, at least ideally, grows out of the unique ex-

[12] "The Poet," *Essays II, Works*, III, 8–10; "Thoreau," *Lectures & Biographical Sketches, Works*, X, 474–476.

perience: "a thought so passionate and alive that like the spirit of
a plant or an animal it has an architecture of its own, and adorns
nature with a new thing." [13]

The idea of form as internal exfoliation parallels Blake's
maxim in *The Marriage of Heaven and Hell:* "Reason is the bound
or outward circumference of Energy," the bounded limits
being merely the demarcation which measures for consciousness
the particular moment's explosive dimensions. Like each symbolic word, the "new thing" which evolves as the poet "resigns
himself to his mood . . . is organic, or the new type which
things themselves take when liberated." Thus while in the
achieved poem "the thought and form are equal in the order of
time," "in the order of genesis the thought is prior to the form."
Translating a sonnet of Michelangelo's, Emerson saw the artist's
hand instinctively drawing out the form hidden but inherent in
the material:

> Never did sculptor's dream unfold
> A form which marble doth not hold
> In its white block; yet it therein shall find
> Only the hand secure and bold
> Which still obeys the mind.

To the end of his life Emerson argued that "rightly, poetry is
organic. We cannot know things by words and writing, but only
by taking a central position in the universe and living in its
forms." [14] Words are not *about* things; they are directly related
to things and so become things in their own right. But like
other things words contain and do not contain, express and do
not express their meaning. If language incarnates spirit, as the

[13] "The Poet," *Essays II, Works,* III, 9–10.
[14] "The Poet," *Essays II, Works,* III, 10, 24; *Poems, Works,* IX, 298;
"Poetry and Imagination," *Letters & Social Aims, Works,* VIII, 42.

axiom in the "Language" chapter of *Nature* says, it does so only pursuant to the Spirit. Words and the form that words assume are consequent upon the seeing:

> This insight, which expresses itself by what is called Imagination, is a very high sort of seeing, which does not come by study, but by the intellect being where and what it sees; by sharing the path or circuit of things through forms, and so making them translucid to others. . . . The condition of true naming, on the poet's part, is his resigning himself to the divine *aura* which breathes through forms, and accompanying that.[15]

The present participles which stitch together all of Emerson's discussions of the poetic process indicate that it is and must be an ongoing process. Achieved forms and stated meanings become fossilized forms and dead meanings. Organic form leads to what has been called more recently "open form" or "composition by field"; and even more specifically it leads to the notion of a poet writing not just long poems or a long poem but a life-poem, its shape acknowledging shapelessness, its lines opening gaps, its meaning sounding the inexhaustibility and indeterminacy of meaning. Emerson's assumptions not only generated Thoreau's journals as well as his own but prefigured Whitman's *Leaves of Grass*, Pound's *Cantos*, Charles Olson's *Maximus Poems*, Robert Duncan's *Passages* and Ginsberg's notebooks in verse and prose.

Emerson could speak in strikingly modern psychological terms of "the projection of God in the unconscious" mind of man, so that the world shows "unconscious truth . . . defined in an object" and thereby brought to expression. In "Bacchus" the poet drinks a "remembering wine" which revives "a dazzling memory" of mythic archetypes. The poetic power is linked re-

---

[15] "The Poet," *Essays II, Works*, III, 26.

peatedly with instinct, spontaneous intuition, dreams, and
"*dream*-power"; and "dream delivers us to dream. . . ." Images
and ideas well up from and lead back to a shared source very
much like the Jungian Collective Unconscious:

> What is the aboriginal Self, on which a universal reliance
> may be grounded? . . . The inquiry leads us to that
> source, at once the essence of genius, of virtue, and of life,
> which we call Spontaneity or Instinct. We denote this pri-
> mary wisdom as Intuition, whilst all later teachings are tu-
> itions. In that deep force, the last fact behind which analy-
> sis cannot go, all things find their common origin. . . . We
> lie in the lap of immense intelligence, which makes us re-
> ceivers of its truth and organs of its activity.[16]

The conception of the poet as seer has, of course, a long history
in western thought from Plato and the Greeks down to the
Romantics of the nineteenth century and on into the twentieth.
But the poet as prophet-seer has adapted himself in particularly
vigorous and bold terms to the New World, in part because
Americans saw themselves as living in more personal and intimate contact with Nature, the primitive source of inspiration,
and in part because the Puritans brought to Nature a strong
sense of its symbolism. Emerson came to his statement of the
idea through his New England heritage—not Puritan theology
but Puritan temperament; and he gave it so American a statement against American acquisitiveness that the reaction down
the decades is still humming today. In fact, the Emersonian
tradition is so strong and deep that Henry Miller, a writer who
one might think is as far removed from Emerson as possible,
speaks of the artistic process in terms which constitute a resumé
of Emerson's principal contentions:

[16] *Nature, NAL, Works,* I, 35, 64–65; "The Poet," *Essays II, Works,*
III, 33, 40; "Self-Reliance," *Essays I, Works,* II, 63–64.

Someone takes over and you just copy out what is being said. . . . A writer shouldn't think much. . . . I'm not very good at thinking. I work from some deep down place; and when I write, well, I don't know just exactly what's going to happen. . . . Who writes the great books? It isn't we who sign our names. What is an artist? He's a man who has antennae, who knows how to hook up to the currents which are in the atmosphere, in the cosmos. . . . Who is original? Everything that we are doing, everything that we think, exists already, and we are intermediaries. . . . [A writer should] recognize himself as a man who was possessed of a certain faculty which he was destined to use for the service of others. He has nothing to be proud of, his name means nothing, his ego is nil, he's only an instrument in a long procession.[17]

In fact, Emerson's sense of the primacy of inspiration and scorn for "rules and particulars" ushered the Dionysian ideal into American literature. The essay on "The Poet" describes him in Dionysian terms—powerful, original, unchained, filled with the god:

there is a great public power on which he can draw, by unlocking, at all risks, his human doors, and suffering the ethereal tides to roll and circulate through him; . . . his speech is thunder, his thought is law. . . . The poet knows that he speaks adequately then only when he speaks somewhat wildly, . . . not with the intellect used as an organ, but with the intellect released from all service and suffered to take its direction from its celestial life; or as the ancients were wont to express themselves, not with intellect alone but with the intellect inebriated by nectar.[18]

[17] *Writers at Work: The Paris Review Interviews, Second Series* (New York, 1963), pp. 171–173.
[18] "The Poet," *Essays II, Works,* III, 3, 26–27; 32 ff., 40.

Emerson's poems are actually not nearly so wild, so drunken, so untrammelled emotionally or metrically as his theory said that poems ideally should be. He was not Whitman, much less Hart Crane, still less Charles Olson or Henry Miller or Ginsberg. He was too gentle and genteel, too fastidious and remote to be a full-blooded and abandoned Dionysian. Even the poem "Bacchus" allows for no misunderstanding from the very first verses: "Bring me wine, but wine which never grew / In the belly of the grape. . . ." And throughout the poem Emerson acceleratingly transcendentalizes the belly-tendencies of his Bacchus. Though sprung "from a nocturnal root," the "leaves and tendrils" of the "true" wine are "curled / Among the silver hills of heaven" and "draw everlasting dew." Through such distillation it becomes the "Wine of Wine" and the "Form of forms" and is finally so rarefied as to become one with the pure Platonic Music of the Spheres: "Wine which Music is,— / Music and Wine are one. . . ." [19]

As Whitman would find out, Emerson was fastidious as well about dwelling on the recognition that the Spirit of Nature moves in sexual rhythms, yet, in this as in so many ways, the way for Whitman was prepared by Emerson. In however modest and unostentatious a manner, the poems move to that rhythm: "The lover watched his graceful maid" ("Each and All"); "And soft perfection of its plan— / Willow and violet, maiden and man" ("May-Day"); "She (Nature) spawneth men as mallows fresh, / Hero and maiden, flesh of her flesh" ("Nature II"); "Primal chimes of sun and shade, / Of sound and echo, man and maid" ("Woodnotes II"); "Sex to sex, and even to odd" ("Ode Inscribed to W. H. Channing"). The following remarkable passage, which opens the second part of "Merlin," is Emer-

[19] *Poems, Works*, IX, 335.

son's most extended and explicit celebration of the sexual life-force to which "Song of Myself" and many subsequent poems would give loud voice:

> The rhyme of the poet
> Modulates the king's affairs;
> Balance-loving Nature
> Made all things in pairs.
> To every foot its antipode;
> Each color with its counter glowed;
> To every tone beat answering tones,
> Higher or graver;
> Flavor gladly blends with flavor;
> Leaf answers leaf upon the bough;
> And match the paired cotyledons.
> Hands to hands, and feet to feet,
> In one body grooms and brides;
> Eldest rite, two married sides
> In every mortal meet.
> Light's far furnace shines,
> Smelting balls and bars,
> Forging double stars,
> Glittering twins and trines.
> The animals are sick with love,
> Lovesick with rhyme;
> Each with all propitious Time
> Into chorus wove.

The anatomical references ("Hands to hands, and feet to feet") identify the body not just as the ground for the individual's union with his sexual complement but also as the vessel for an androgynous consciousness within the individual, which further deepens his capacity for union: "In one body grooms and brides; / Eldest rite, two married sides / In every mortal meet."

It is true that this is an uncharacteristically full-bodied moment in Emerson. He could at times see in himself the disembodied remoteness that even his friends complained of; he regretted to his journal that "the chief defect of my nature" was "the want of animal spirits" and admitted in other journal entries: "I was born cold. My bodily habit is cold. I shiver in and out. . ."; and again, "Even for those whom I really love I have not animal spirits." It is not difficult to see why he shrunk from what seemed to him the vulgarity and coarseness that Whitman came to display in some poems, and why he had only harsh reproof for those would-be Dionysians who tried to induce vision with drugs, drink, and other sensual stimulants. Since "wine, mead, narcotics, coffee, tea, opium, the fumes of sandalwood and tobacco" are "*quasi*-mechanical substitutes for the true nectar," such "counterfeit excitement and fury" can end only in "dissipation and deterioration." [20]

Nonetheless, Emerson's advocacy of the Dionysian ideal could not have been more crucial for the course of American poetry. Emerson's informing presence made him, in fact, a chief target for twentieth-century poet-critics—Eliot, Allen Tate, Yvor Winters—who wanted to exorcise the deep, abiding influence of Romanticism. They disapproved of and dismissed Romanticism on moral and psychological as well as artistic grounds; they feared, in themselves as well as in others, that its individualism, its openness to the impulses of experience, its sourcing of inspiration in the emotions and the unconscious led to solipsism, madness, suicide. For a critic like Winters, Emerson was particularly insidious because he made Romanticism seem sane and wholesome, and it was not enough for Winters to

[20] *The Heart of Emerson's Journals*, ed. Bliss Perry (Boston, 1926), pp. 204, 33, 215; "The Poet," *Essays II, Works*, III, 27–29. See also "Circles," *Essays I, Works*, II, 322.

note that he did not "practice what he preaches." He could say "Of Poe and Whitman, the less said the better" and take that assertion as fairly self-evident; Tate agreed that the disastrous influence of both sealed Hart Crane's doom. But Winters' inverted acknowledgment of Emerson is expressed in his inveighing against Emerson "in defense of reason" with an urgent conviction that Emerson was his most dangerous adversary in America.[21]

Emerson may not have fully practiced what he preached, but his importance lies in the fact that he did state the principles and begin the experiments. He stands, nervous and self-conscious in the role, as our teetotalling Bacchus, our New England and ministerial Pan. Now we can see that his experiments were only a point of departure for later poets, heralding Whitman's free verse, Pound's and Williams' innovations with speech rhythms and breath units and open forms, E. E. Cummings' refashioning of syntax and punctuation and typography, Charles Olson's "projective verse," Denise Levertov's organic form, the long lines and cumulative periods of Robinson Jeffers, William Everson, and Allen Ginsberg. Most of these poets, after Whitman, would not have shared with Emerson the metaphysics which was the basis for his poetics. But the metaphysical, even transcendental, impulse has remained active, even though more cautiously and circumspectly in many cases—in Pound's Platonism and his indebtedness, especially in the theory of form and language, to Ernest Fenollosa, who was himself teaching in Japan the Transcendentalist philosophy he had imbibed at Harvard; in Cummings' devotion to his father, a Unitarian minister with a strong Emersonian spirit; in Jeffers' Calvinist pantheism;

---

[21] Yvor Winters, *In Defense of Reason* (New York, 1947), p. 55; "Critical Foreword," *The Complete Poems of Frederick Goddard Tuckerman*, ed. N. Scott Momaday (New York, 1965), p. ix.

in Olson's response to Carl Jung's archetypal psychology and A. N. Whitehead's process philosophy; in Duncan's fascination with myth and mysticism; in Levertov, through her father, a Jew steeped in Hasidic thought who became a Christian and an Anglican priest; in Ginsberg's Judaic, Oriental, and Blakean spirit; in Everson's fusion of Christian theology and Jungian psychology. As a result, most of these poets have viewed the poet as a special seer, and all of them, as at least a special perceiver. Their various explorations of ongoing form and emergent structure have been grounded, for all of them, in the organic yet transcendent process of nature. Along with other poets akin in spirit they comprise the distinctive strain of the American poetic tradition, and Emerson is their source, more than some of them have wished to acknowledge and more than Emerson himself could have foreseen.

The Program

Saturday, August 31, Through Tuesday, September 3, 1974

I. THE LITERATURE OF FACT

Directed by E. D. Hirsch, Jr., The University of Virginia
Sat.	1:45 P.M.	The Torment of the Particular
		Robert Nisbet, Columbia University
Sun.	9:30 A.M.	Substance and Form in Social History
		David H. Fischer, Brandeis University
Sun.	11:00 A.M.	Art and Factual Testimony
		Paul Fussell, Jr., Rutgers University

II. EMERSON ONCE MORE

Directed by David Levin, The University of Virginia
Sat.	3:15 P.M.	Emerson: The Paradox of Organic Form
		Albert J. Gelpi, Stanford University
Sun.	1:45 P.M.	Emerson, England, and Fate
		Phyllis Cole, Wellesley College
Sun.	3:15 P.M.	Emerson and the American Metamorphosis
		Daniel B. Shea, Jr., Washington University

III. IMITATION, PLAGIARISM, AND INFLUENCE

Directed by Thomas McFarland, The City University of New York
Mon.	9:30 A.M.	The Renaissance Artist as Plagiarist
		Stephen Orgel, The University of California, Berkeley
Mon.	11:00 A.M.	Wordsworth and Coleridge: Influence and Confluence
		J. B. Beer, Peterhouse, The University of Cambridge
Tues.	9:30 A.M.	Formalism, Savagery, and Care; Or, The Function of Criticism Once Again
		Jerome McGann, The University of Chicago
Tues.	11:00 A.M.	A Meditation on Belatedness, and a Synopsis
		Harold Bloom, Yale University

IV.   REVALUATIONS OF VIRGINIA WOOLF

Directed by Ralph Freedman, Princeton University

Mon.   1:45 P.M.   Hunting the Moth: Virginia Woolf and the Creative Imagination
Harvena Richter, The University of New Mexico

Mon.   3:15 P.M.   Dark Lady or Sonnets: The Role of Biography in
the Criticism of Virginia Woolf
Quentin Bell, The University of Sussex

Tues.   1:45 P.M.   Forms of the Woolfian Short Story
Avrom Fleishman, The Johns Hopkins University

Tues.   3:15 P.M.   History and Narrative in *Between the Acts*
J. Hillis Miller, Yale University

Ruth M. Adams, Dartmouth College; Alan Akmakjian, Royal Oak, Michigan; Marcia Allentuck, City University of New York; Paul Alpers, University of California at Berkeley; Valborg Anderson, Brooklyn College; Hugh B. Andrews, Northern Michigan University

George W. Bahlke, Kirkland College; Heather Banks, University of Maryland; James E. Barcus, Houghton College; Jonas A. Barish, University of California at Berkeley; J. Robert Barth, S.J., University of Missouri; Bertrice Bartlett, Stephens College; Bruce Bashford, State University of New York at Stony Brook; John E. Becker, Fairleigh Dickinson University; John Beer, University of Cambridge; Millicent Bell, Boston University; Warner Berthoff, Harvard University; J. Thomas Bertrand, University of Virginia; Murray Biggs, Massachusetts Institute of Technology; Kenneth A. Bleeth, Boston University; Charles Blyth, Cambridge, Massachusetts; Anne C. Bolgan, University of Western Ontario; W. F. Bolton, Douglass College, Rutgers University; George J. Bornstein, University of Michigan; John D. Boyd, S.J., Fordham University; Frank Brady, City University of New York; Leo Braudy, Columbia University; Martha M. Briney, Hood College; Marianne Brock, Mount Holyoke College; Leonora Leet Brodwin, St. John's University; Stanley Brodwin, Hofstra University; Candace Brook, Harvard University; Judith Gwyn Brown, New York, New York; Lawrence Buell, Oberlin College; Daniel Burke, F.S.C., La Salle College; Mervin Butovsky, Sir George Williams University

Daniel J. Cahill, University of Northern Iowa; Ruth A. Cameron, Eastern Nazarene College; Eric W. Carlson, University of Connecticut; Julia L. Carlson, University of Maine at Orono; Thomas R. Carper, University of Maine at Portland-Gorham; Robert L. Caserio, State University of New York at Buffalo; Thomas H. Calfant, Alabama State University; Edward D. Clarke, Sr., Fayetteville State University; James L. Clifford, Columbia University; Phyllis Cole, Wellesley College; M. Donald Coleman, Mamaroneck, New York; Arthur N. Collins, State University of New York at Albany; Craig Comstock, Stanford University; Peggy Comstock, Stanford University; Frederick W. Conner, University of Alabama in Birmingham; Marian Connor, Roxbury Community College; Albert S. Cook, State University of New York at Buffalo; Philip Cooper, University of Maryland Baltimore County; Patricia Craddock, Boston University; G. Armour Craig, Amherst College; J. Donald Crowley, University of Missouri at Columbia; J. V. Cunningham, Brandeis University

Emily K. Dalgarno, Boston University; Cynthia D'Ambrosio, Hollins College; Vinne-Marie D'Ambrosio, Brooklyn College, City University of New York; Ruth E. Danon, University of Connecticut; Irene Dash, Hunter College, City University of New York; Winifred M. Davis, Columbia University; Robert Adams Day, City University of New York; Joanne T. Dempsey, Vassar College; Constance Ayers Denne, Baruch College, City University of New York; C. J. Denne, Jr., College of New Rochelle; Joanne Feit Diehl, Yale University; Thomas F. Dillingham, Stephens College; Evelyn C. Dodge, Framingham Center, Massachusetts; Muriel Dollar, Caldwell College; Stephen L. Donadio, Columbia University; E. Talbot Donaldson, Indiana University; Sister Rose Bernard Donna, C.S.J., The College of Saint Rose; Sharon S. Doten, Boston University; Anne T. Doyle, Mount Holyoke College; Danny Ducker, Millersville State College; Georgia Dunbar, Hofstra University

Thomas R. Edwards, Rutgers University; David A. Ellis, Tufts University; Monroe Engel, Harvard University; Edward Engelberg, Brandeis University; Martha W. England, Queens College of the City University of New York; David Erdman, State University of New York and New York Public Library; Sister Marie Eugénie, Immaculata College

D. Paul Farr, Greenville, North Carolina; Mrs. D. Paul Farr, Greenville, North Carolina; Frances C. Ferguson, The Johns Hopkins University; Moira Ferguson, Stockton State College; David Ferry, Wellesley College; Stanley Fish, The Johns Hopkins University; Philip Fisher, Brandeis University; Avrom Fleishman, The Johns Hopkins University; Agnus Fletcher, City University of New York; Dean

Flower, Smith College; Leslie D. Foster, Northern Michigan University; Richard Lee Francis, Western Washington State College; Georgine F. Freedman, Princeton, New Jersey; Ralph Freedman, Princeton University; Warren French, Indiana University; Albert B. Friedman, Claremont Graduate School; Northrop Frye, University of Toronto; Margaretta Fulton, Harvard University Press; Paul Fussell, Jr., Rutgers University

Margaret E. Gage, Amherst, Massachusetts; Dewey Ganzel, Oberlin College; Burdett H. Gardner, Monmouth College; Harry R. Garvin, Bucknell University; Marilyn Gaull, Temple University; Blanche H. Gelfant, Dartmouth College; Albert J. Gelpi, Stanford University; Barbara Gill, Emmanuel College; Harry Girling, York University; Alex Gold, Jr., Boston University; Arnold Goldman, Vassar College; David J. Gordon, Hunter College, City University of New York; Gerald T. Gordon, University of Maine; Susan R. Gorsky, Cleveland State University; J. W. Graham, University of Western Ontario; Dr. James Gray, Dalhousie University; Evelyn Barish Greenberger, Staten Island Community College; Ernest G. Griffin, York University; Allen K. Grossman, Brandeis University; Allen Guttmann, Amherst College

Claire Hahn, Fordham University; Sarah C. Hall, The Polytechnic School; Violet Beryl Halpert, Fairleigh Dickinson University; Victor Harris, Brandeis University; Phillip Harth, University of Wisconsin; Geoffrey Hartman, Yale University; Joan E. Hartman, Staten Island Community College; Miriam M. Heffernan, Brooklyn College; Suzette A. Henke, University of Virginia; Margaret Higonnet, University of Connecticut; James L. Hill, Michigan State University; William B. Hill, S.J., University of Scranton; Howard H. Hinkel, University of Missouri; E. D. Hirsch, Jr., University of Virginia; Fred C. Hobson, Jr., University of Alabama; C. Fenno Hoffman, Jr., Rhode Island School of Design; Daniel Hoffman, University of Pennsylvania; Laurence B. Holland, The Johns Hopkins University; Myra C. Holmes, University of Connecticut; Vivian C. Hopkins, State University of New York at Albany; Chaviva Hošek, Victoria College, University of Tornoto; Donald Howard, The Johns Hopkins University; John F. Hulcoop, University of British Columbia; Jean M. Humez, Boston University; Madeline Hummel, Kresge College, University of California; Lawrence Hyman, Brooklyn College, City University of New York; Virginia Hyman, Newark College, Rutgers University; Samuel Hynes, Northwestern University

Nora Crow Jaffe, Smith College; Richard A. Johnson, Mount Holyoke College

Walter Kaiser, Harvard University; Deborah Kaplan, Brandeis University; Marjorie Kaufman, Mount Holyoke College; Donald Kay, University of Alabama; Norman Kelvin, City College, City University of New York; Rudolf Kirk, Rutgers University; Diana J. Kleiner, Brookline, Massachusetts; H. L. Kleinfield, C. W. Post, Long Island University; Theodora J. Koob, Shippensburg State College

J. Craig La Drière, Harvard University; Robert Langbaum, University of Virginia; Jon Lanham, Northeastern University; Penelope Laurans, Yale University; Lewis Leary, University of North Carolina; David Levin, University of Virginia; Thomas S. W. Lewis, Skidmore College; Dwight N. Lindley, Hamilton College; Lawrence Lipking, Princeton University; A. Walton Litz, Princeton University; Joseph P. Lovering, Canisius College; Sister Alice Lubin, College of Saint Elizabeth

Isabel G. MacCaffrey, Harvard University; Paul Magnuson, New York University; Jane Marcus, State University of New York; Daniel Marder, University of Tulsa; William McBrian, Hofstra University; John McDiarmid, St. Anselm's College; Lucy S. McDiarmid, Swarthmore College; Stuart Y. McDougal, University of Michigan; George F. McFarland, St. Lawrence University; Thomas McFarland, City University of New York; Jerome McGann, University of Chicago; Terence J. McKenzie, U.S. Coast Guard Academy; Thomas M. McLaughlin, Temple University; Donald A. McQuade, Queens College, City University of New York; Donald C. Mell, University of Delaware; Sister Jean Memmer, College of St. Elizabeth; Eilis Dillon Mercier, Dublin, Ireland; Vivian H. S. Mercier, University of California at Santa Barbara; Lore Metzger, Emory University; Selma Meyerowitz, Wayne State University; John H. Middendorf, Columbia University; Barbara Miliaras, Lowell Technological Institute; Dr. Louis T. Milic, Cleveland State University; J. Hillis Miller, Yale University; Francis Murphy, Smith College

Tohru Nakamura, Ibaraki University, Japan; Jack L. Nelson, Agnes Scott College; Lowry Nelson, Jr., Yale University; Margaret Neussendorfer, University of Texas, Permian Basin; Robert Nisbet, Columbia University; Donald R. Noble, University of Alabama; Marjorie Norris, City University of New York; Jane Dailey Novak, University of East Anglia

Elaine R. Ognibene, Siena College; Carol Burke Ohmann, Wesleyan University; Richard Ohmann, Wesleyan University; James Olney, North Carolina Central University; Stephen Orgel, University of California at Berkeley; James M. Osborn, Yale University; Chas. A. Owen, Jr., University of Connecticut; Patricia Owen, Lehman College, City University of New York

Stephen Parrish, Cornell University; Ronald Paulson, The Johns Hopkins University; Roy Harvey Pearce, University of California at San Diego; Norman Holmes Pearson, Yale University; Henry H. Peyton III, Memphis State University; Anne H. Phillips, U.S. Naval Academy; Esther Whitmarsh Phillips, Vassar College; William Phillips, Partisan Review; Burton Pike, Queens College, City University of New York; Nicholas S. Poburko, Dalhousie University; Richard Podgorski, Pace University; Joel Porte, Harvard University; Kathleen Porter, St. Lawrence University; Robert O. Preyer, Brandeis University; Ruth Prigozy, Hofstra University

Joseph A. Quinn, University of Windsor

Grace Radin, City University of New York; Shaista Rahman, Brooklyn College, City University of New York; David Rampton, Vancouver, Canada; Joan Reardon, Barat College; Donald H. Reiman, The Carl H. Pforzheimer Library; ·Harvena Richter, University of New Mexico; Keith N. Richwine, Western Maryland College; Harriet Ritvo, Harvard University; John R. Roberts, University of Missouri; Jeffrey Robinson, University of Colorado; Phil Rogers, Queen's University; E. J. Rose, University of Alberta; Phyllis Rose, Wesleyan University; Shirley Rose, University of Alberta; J. Carter Rowland, State University College; Nancy A. Rozanski, University of Connecticut; Lucio P. Ruotolo, Stanford University; Roberta Russell, University of Connecticut

Irene Samuel, Emory University; Miyoko Sasaki, Tsuda College, Japan; Helene B. M. Schnabel, Manhattan, New York; Harry T.

Schultz, Dartmouth College; Richard J. Sexton, Fordham University; Elinor Stoneman Shaffer, Cambridge, England; Harold I. Shapiro, University of North Carolina; Daniel B. Shea, Jr., Washington University; Elaine Showalter, Douglass College, Rutgers University; Frank Shuffelton, University of Rochester; William Sievert, Pace University; C. Anderson Silber, Victoria College, University of Toronto; Patricia L. Skarda, Smith College; A. Helen Smith, Siena College; Alexander Smith, Jr., University of Connecticut; Carol Smith, Douglass College, Rutgers University; Sarah W. R. Smith, Harvard University; Susan Sutton Smith, State University of New York College at Oneonta; Blair R. Sorrel, Smith College; Mark Spilka, Brown University; Robert E. Spiller, University of Pennsylvania; Hugh Sproule, Dalhousie University; Rhoda McCord Staley, State University of New York at Stony Brook; Thomas F. Staley, University of Tulsa; Elizabeth Steele, University of Toledo; Arnold Stein, The Johns Hopkins University; Marion L. Stein, State University of New York at Stony Brook; A. Wilber Stevens, University of Nevada at Las Vegas; Holly Stevens, Yale University; Albert Stone, Jr., Hellenic College; Gary Lee Stonum, Case Western Reserve University; Jean Sudrann, Mount Holyoke College; Maureen Sullivan, Marquette University; P. Leon Surette, University of Western Ontario; Deborah E. Swain, University of North Carolina at Chapel Hill; Donald R. Swanson, Wright State University

Robert D. Thornton, State University of New York at New Paltz; Ruth Z. Temple, City University of New York; Margaret G. Trotter, Agnes Scott College; Lewis A. Turlish, Bates College

Virginia W. Valentine, University of South Florida at Tampa; Marie-Claire Van Der Elst, Paris III, France; Helen Vendler, Boston University; Howard P. Vincent, Kent State University; Thomas A. Vogler, University of California at Santa Cruz

Eugene M. Waith, Yale University; Melissa G. Walker, Mercer University in Atlanta; Emily M. Wallace, Philadelphia, Pennsylvania; Aileen Ward, Brandeis University; John Pierce Watkins, California State College; Sister Mary Anthony Weinig, Rosemont College; Barry L. Weller, The Johns Hopkins University; Ronald A. Wells, U.S. Coast Guard Academy; Laura Wexler, Columbia University; Robert O.

White, Massachusetts College of Pharmacy; Joseph Wiesenfarth, University of Wisconsin at Madison; Maurita Willett, University of Illinois, Chicago Circle; Rea Wilmshurst, Toronto, Canada; William K. Wimsatt, Yale University; M. L. Wine, University of Illinois, Chicago Circle; Donald J. Winslow, Boston University; Hana Wirth-Nesher, Columbia University; Philip Withim, Bucknell University; Dorothy M. Woldt, Oshkosh, Wisconsin; Michael Wood, Columbia University; Samuel K. Workman, Newark College of Engineering; Mildred Worthington, Bentley College

Jan Young, Skidmore College